The Geoeconomics of Global Value Chains

The post-Cold War era was widely associated with the Washington Consensus, which promoted economic efficiency, specialization, and trade liberalization as pathways to growth and social welfare. Globalization facilitated the rise of geographically dispersed production networks, known as global value chains (GVCs). For decades, firms benefited from offshoring by exploiting labour cost differentials, accessing cheaper resources, and entering new markets. However, since 2010, political and societal shifts have driven a collective reconfiguration of GVCs. Today, manufacturing systems are being reshaped by three major forces: digital transformation, climate change, and geopolitical tensions.

This volume focuses on the latter – geopolitical disruptions – and examines their impact on corporate strategies related to trade and foreign direct investment. Firms increasingly respond by relocating operations, either through reshoring to the home country or through nearshoring to adjacent regions. The study investigates the drivers behind these decisions, comparing current reshoring patterns with previous disruptions, such as those during the COVID-19 pandemic. It also evaluates the role of policy frameworks in enabling relocation and considers how these may evolve. While the analysis centres on the European Union, it offers a global perspective on geopolitical risks. The book serves as a key resource for academics, practitioners, and policymakers seeking to understand international business and investment decisions.

Katarzyna Mroczek-Dąbrowska is an international business scholar and the Head of the Department of International Competitiveness at the Poznań University of Economics and Business, Poland. She specializes in international competitiveness, economic policy, resilience, and global business strategy, particularly in the context of geopolitical and economic disruptions.

Routledge Focus on Economics and Finance

The fields of economics are constantly expanding and evolving. This growth presents challenges for readers trying to keep up with the latest important insights. Routledge Focus on Economics and Finance presents short books on the latest big topics, linking in with the most cutting-edge economics research.

Individually, each title in the series provides coverage of a key academic topic, whilst collectively the series forms a comprehensive collection across the whole spectrum of economics.

Financial Resilience and the Sustainable Development Goals
Edited by Magdalena Zioło and Bruno S. Sergi

Geopolitics, China, and the Global Supply Chain
Issues and Implications
Sarah Chan

Proactivity in Economics
Between Resourcefulness and Entrepreneurship
Jakub Bożydar Wiśniewski

The Geoeconomics of Global Value Chains
Navigating Geopolitical Complexity and Industrial Policy Shifts
Katarzyna Mroczek-Dąbrowska

For more information about this series, please visit: www.routledge.com/Routledge-Focus-on-Economics-and-Finance/book-series/RFEF

The Geoeconomics of Global Value Chains

Navigating Geopolitical Complexity and Industrial Policy Shifts

Katarzyna Mroczek-Dąbrowska

Routledge
Taylor & Francis Group
LONDON AND NEW YORK

First published 2026
by Routledge
4 Park Square, Milton Park, Abingdon, Oxon OX14 4RN

and by Routledge
605 Third Avenue, New York, NY 10158

Routledge is an imprint of the Taylor & Francis Group, an informa business

British Library Cataloguing-in-Publication Data
A catalogue record for this book is available from the British Library

ISBN: 978-1-041-20905-8 (hbk)
ISBN: 978-1-041-20907-2 (pbk)
ISBN: 978-1-003-72480-3 (ebk)

DOI: 10.4324/9781003724803

Typeset in Times New Roman
by Newgen Publishing UK

To my Sons

Contents

Data availability statement

The data that support the findings of this book/chapter are available from the author, upon reasonable request.

1 Global value chains

On a lookout for rewiring?

To many the post-Cold War Washington Consensus emerged as a synonym of a new era where economic efficiency and specialization would lead to liberalization of global trade, economic growth, and social warfare. The globalization proved to be the driver to create geographically dispersed networks that we know as the GVCs (Baldwin, 2016). For decades companies ripped the benefits of offshored operations, taking advantage of the labour cost gap, exploiting cheaper resources, and penetrating new markets. Yet, since around 2010, the changes in politics and society have been pushing for collective rewiring of the GVCs. The contemporary transformation of manufacturing systems and rewiring of the GVCs is triggered by three disruptive megatrends: digital transformation, climate change, and geopolitical tensions (World Economic Forum, 2024). The undisputable climate change is evidenced in both extensive flooding, widespread droughts, and intensifying temperature raise which in turn affect the delivery routes and times. So do geopolitical conflicts that render certain regions undesirable to invest in or uphold relationships with. Political animosities lead to forming blocks, increasing risk, and fuelling tensions. Technological advancement on the other hand can present both opportunity – by enhancing performance and efficiency – as well as threat by spreading disinformation and data breaches. The configuration of the manufacturing processes has shifted from performance-oriented one to an approach where companies need to leverage performance, resilience, and sustainability.

The redesign of the GVCs is also attributed to features of the contemporary world often characterized as the VUCA world. VUCA is an acronym, reflecting on volatility, uncertainty, complexity and

DOI: 10.4324/9781003724803-1

ambiguity of the contemporary world we live in. Volatility means that a certain process is unexpected or unstable, and we might not predict its duration. Uncertainty means that we lack information on it and that the event's basic cause and effect remain unknown. Complexity means that the situation has interconnected parts and factors. Finally, ambiguity means that the situation has no precedents and casual relationships are unknown. In response to the VUCA framework Cascio (2020) coined the term "BANI world" which is expected to better capture the complexity of contemporary disruptions. The world is seen as: brittle, i.e. fragile, susceptible to breaking and almost chaotic; anxious, i.e. pertaining in constant state of uncertainty and unease; non-linear, i.e. remains non-sequential without evident cause-and-effect patterns and mechanisms; and finally incomprehensible, i.e. unpredictable, overloaded with information that remain unprocessable. The BANI (Brittle, Anxious, Non-linear, and Incomprehensible) framework also seems to describe the GVCs well. The GVCs are brittle as the "black swans" have been known to cause immediate failures and bottlenecks in the interconnected system. The companies remain anxious over forthcoming changes and regulations, those expected (e.g. beforementioned megatrends), and unexpected ones. They are also becoming nonlinear with operations being carried out simultaneously, hence increasing the complexity of the manufacturing process. Finally, they are increasingly incomprehensible as decision makers lack reliable reference points and information thus becoming prone to making subjective, "gut-feeling" choices.

The concept of a value chain encompasses all key steps companies undertake to develop a product or to deliver a service – from generating the idea to its final consumption and even beyond. The process covers various stages, including: design, manufacturing, marketing activities, customer support and others. The activities within a value chain can be either performed by multiple companies or can be kept in-house but dispersed across countries, hence the label "global" that is attributed to the value chains (Brennan & Rakhmatullin, 2017). GVCs embody the essence of globalization, which fundamentally involves the movement of materials, goods, data, know-how, capital, and employees. In turn, the continuous process of rethinking and redesigning of the GVCs amplifies the globalization's impact itself.

Although the benefits of increased trade integration are undeniable, we also observe changes to the GVCs that have made them more complex. On the one hand, emerging economies entered the path of income convergence, firms enjoy higher productivity and consumers wider choice of goods but on the other, countries became more dependent on one another with production of some key items limited to specific countries and sometimes even firms (Islam & Chadee, 2024). Some characteristics of GVCs as well external circumstances have caused the GVCs to experience a number of choke points (bottlenecks), i.e. locations or agents that disrupt the flow of goods and information. These vulnerabilities have contemporary been caused by:

- external shocks that now mostly relate to geopolitical disruptions and COVID-19 pandemic; the geopolitical disruptions encompass wide array of events, from wars and regional armed conflicts, through threats stemming from political instability to existing supply restrictions and trade sanctions,
- "secondary" shocks, e.g. transportation disruptions; generally transportation networks suffer as a consequence of another disruption and are short-lived. Yet their impact on GVCs is significantly affecting their resilience as shipping networks are limited to a small set of routes and lack viable alternatives (Heiland et al., 2022),
- GVC structure and governance – the frictions between the production network and supplier network as well as the degree of the concentration vs diversification can affect the GVCs performance in case of any change,
- GVC substitutability degree – the degree to which GVCs structure could be easily changed by substituting entities providing certain input,
- GVC complementarity degree – the degree to which GVCs structure is dependent on the output in another GVC (e.g. semiconductors, electricity, gas).

It is expected that in the near future the sustainability-related goals, i.e. transition towards climate-neutral economy will also significantly impact the structure of the GVCs (De Marchi & Gereffi, 2023). Raw materials will be in high demand, with OECD (2019) predicting their overall global usage to double by 2060. In effect, coupled with geopolitical shifts, the GVC structures may undergo a substantial reconfiguration. For a long time literature has supported the notion that GVCs were constantly reconfiguring with the attempt to boost companies' competitiveness (Pananond et al., 2020; Rodriguez et al., 2023). The most commonly assumed changes involved relocation decisions, supplier diversification, discontinuation of certain activities and shifts in the GVCs' governance modes (Strange & Humphrey, 2019). These decisions were seen as natural consequence to market changes, e.g. new market entrants or digitalization when new GVC structure would benefit from altered arrangements.

Yet, for instance, the impact of COVID-19 pandemic on reshoring trend proved to be much lesser than anticipated (Dachs et al., 2019; Kano et al., 2022; Mroczek-Dąbrowska et al., 2024). The changes were short-lived and did not lead to structural redesign of the value chain activities. The nature of the managerial responses to the global megatrends might however be different. Climate concerns, geopolitical tensions, and technological advancement are expected to exert a systemic change including governance adaptation, concentration, length, and geographical dispersion of the GVC structure. Additionally, the COVID-19 pandemic has added another feature to how the GVC rewiring may unfold – will GVCs become more resilient to the changing environment? And the question remains whether resilience can go in hand with competitiveness or is it rather a choice between resilient or competitive GVCs.

GVCs stimulate company's competitive advantage by merging both local and competitive edges, including unique firm advantages and location-specific strengths. In the contemporary landscape of competition, where the rivalry is shifting from interfirm to inter-GVCs power struggle, it is essential to cultivate and preserve a GVC's competitive nature. Therefore, GVCs should focus on developing sustainable competitive advantages by creating distinctive dynamic capabilities (Ascani et al., 2020). Yet, as we observe increased impact of global disruptions on the various economic activities, the discussion on GVCs seems to be shifting from making the GVCs *competitive* to making them *resilient*. Scopus database indicates a notable switch in the number of publications focusing on the two terms (Figure 1.1; 2022 onwards). While research on competitiveness remains strong, there is an equal interest in building resilience capabilities of different systems.

It is still debatable whether competitive (or efficient) and resilient GVCs are mutually exclusive. Galston (2020) claims that global economic system has proven efficient in finding the optimal adaptation to the existing circumstances yet fails to adapt to unexpected disruptions waiting in the future, hence putting the terms *efficiency* and *resilience* at odds. This can be proved by the concept of "slack resources" which

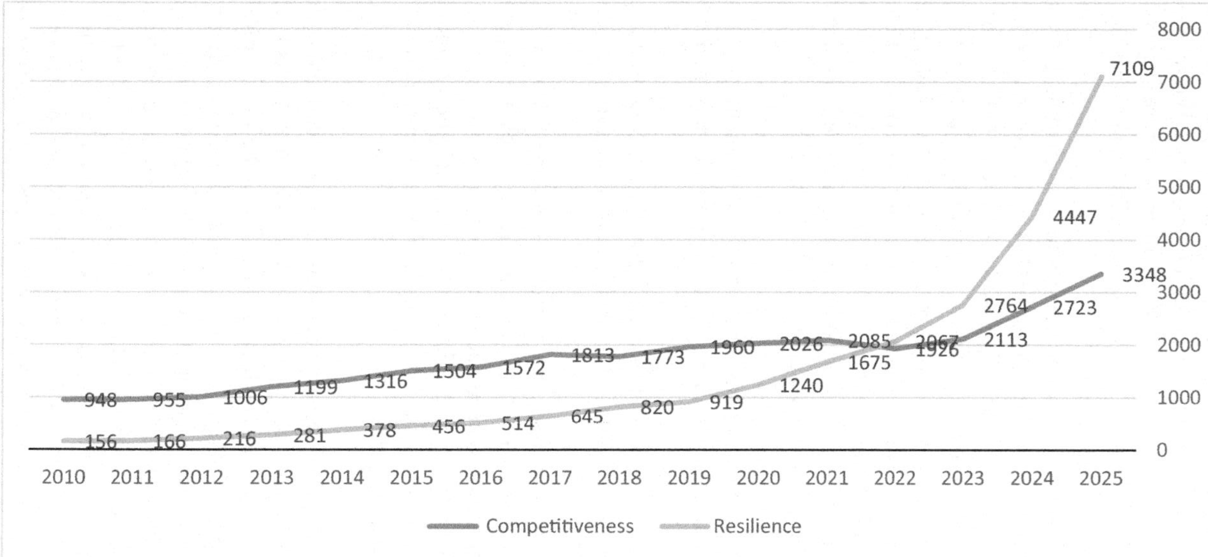

Figure 1.1 Competitiveness vs resilience – number of documents published 2010–2025.

Note: Search limited to areas of Business, Management and Accounting and Economics, Econometrics and Finance, publication type: articles and book chapters.

Source: Own elaboration based on Scopus database.

on the one hand increase operational costs and reduce company's efficiency but at the same time serve as a buffer in an event of crisis boosting the resilience capabilities (Pettit et al., 2010). While in short run this is true, Gölgeci et al. (2020) claim that both resilience and effectiveness, as well as diversity, adaptability, and cohesion are needed to create durable systems.

Against the backdrop of ongoing debates surrounding the trade-offs between efficiency and resilience in GVCs, this volume examines the evolving patterns of reconfiguration and their implications for companies. The main objective of the research is to identify the primary trajectories that the GVCs follow in response to escalating geopolitical tensions. Within the broader context of the BANI world and the influence of global megatrends, there is growing pressure to rewire established production structures. With the reconfiguration come certain research questions, this volume intends to explore:

- RQ1: To what extent are relocation strategies – including reshoring, nearshoring, and friendshoring – prevalent in the ongoing restructuring of GVCs?
- RQ2: What are the key antecedents driving relocation strategies in the context of geopolitical instability, and how are these factors interrelated?
- RQ3: How do firms assess the usefulness of data-driven decision-making models and in what ways can these models be integrated into their relocation-related decision-making process?
- RQ4: In what ways does the European legal and policy framework facilitate the reconfiguration of production systems, particularly through relocation pathway?

Each of the proposed research questions is interlinked and collectively forms a coherent line of inquiry. Together, they contribute to the main aim of the study, which is to identify the most prevalent strategies companies adopt to face the need for reconfiguring their operations in response to geopolitical pressures. The ongoing debate around relocation strategies remains unresolved, suggesting that reshoring is still under-utilized. However, relocation – although not used as dominantly as had been anticipated – has gained momentum in recent years. This observation justifies RQ1, which explores the extent to which relocation strategies such as reshoring, nearshoring, and friendshoring are currently employed.

Following this, the question arises as to how geopolitical instability – one of today's key megatrends – shapes relocation strategies. What truly drives these decisions? Under what conditions can one anticipate relocation, and how do changes in one variable (e.g., political risk, regulatory burden) affect others? Is there a predictable set of circumstances that leads to reshoring or alternative forms of relocation? These questions lead to RQ2, which investigates the main antecedents of relocation strategies and the interdependence of influencing factors. If such a model of relocation determinants can be established, it becomes crucial to assess whether companies can implement it effectively. Can data-driven models be integrated into corporate decision-making, offering a blueprint for strategic relocation? This gives rise to RQ3, which examines the applicability of such models in practice.

Finally, attention must be given to policy. Is the European legal and policy framework conducive to supporting relocation strategies? Is it aligned with firms' needs, or does it lag behind? How does it compare globally? These considerations inform RQ4, which evaluates the policy implications of relocation dynamics and the potential for empirical insights to shape future regulatory frameworks. The monograph in question presents a comprehensive and multilayered exploration of the impact of geopolitical shifts on GVCs, with a particular focus on reconfiguration strategies and policy responses within the European context. Its structure has been designed to answer the abovementioned research questions. It reflects a logical progression from a high-level diagnosis of the global geopolitical environment to detailed case study and conceptual clarifications, ultimately culminating in policy analysis and regulations. Each chapter builds upon the previous, offering both theoretical frameworks and empirical analyses. The monograph consists of eight chapters, including the introduction and final reflections.

Chapter 2 titled 'The three "de-"s – global economy in face of geopolitical complexity' sets the analytical backbone of the monograph by introducing the current state of the global economy through the lens of three interrelated trends: deglobalization, decoupling, and de-risking. These concepts are central to understanding the monograph's subsequent parts as the empirical analyses are set against the backdrop of the current economic and geopolitical dynamics. The chapter opens by identifying most up-to-date geopolitical risks GVCs are currently facing, including armed conflicts, disrupted shipment arrangements, international trade, and investment shifts as well as election cycles. The rollout of these disruptions illustrates how vulnerable and exposed the interconnected GVCs can become in times of instability. Institutional weaknesses are then examined, suggesting that long-standing global frameworks may be ill-equipped to handle emerging geopolitical pressures. Finally, the chapter introduces the concept of a "multipolar global economy", suggesting a shift away from U.S.- or China-centered dynamics to a more complex geopolitical configuration. The final sub-section addresses the growing interplay between geopolitical alignment and investment patterns, which constitutes the basis for the empirical reconfiguration analysis that follows in subsequent chapters.

Chapter 3 titled 'Global value chains and megatrends' provides the conceptual grounding for the monograph. The chapter introduces the GVC paradigm, a well-established conceptual framework in international economics that captures the fragmentation and global dispersion of production. The phenomenon is however highly affected by the three contemporary megatrends: technological transformation, sustainability pressures, and geopolitical realignment which may significantly alter the long-term trajectories of production networks. Based on systematic literature review, the study identifies a gap in the literature concerning how these megatrends intersect with geopolitics, effectively setting up the research questions and rationale for the following empirical investigations.

The empirical core of the monograph begins with Chapter 4 titled 'Geopolitical distress and GVCs' resilience – towards reconfiguration?' The study discusses how "geopolitical turmoil" is actively reshaping the logic and structure of GVCs, prompting firms to explore "reconfiguration strategies" to enhance resilience. It explores the experiences of Central and Eastern European companies that are embedded in global GVCs and have undertaken different pathways in adapting to the increasing uncertainty. The European landscape is analysed in detail, reflecting the region's struggle to balance efficiency with security amid rising geopolitical tensions. The results of the analysis highlights the path dependency of reconfiguration pathways, emphasizing how previous decisions significantly influence current choices of the firms. The chapter presents early evidence on the trends, patterns, and constraints firms face when reconfiguring their GVCs. One of the pathways explored is the relocation strategy, which antecedents will be examined in detail in the following chapter.

Chapter 5 titled 'Relocation as a GVC reconfiguration trajectory' is the exemplification of one of the strategic reconfiguration pathways that were identified in Chapter 4. It starts with conceptual and methodological overview of relocation, defining related terms and outlining company's motivations for such adaptive strategy. The chapter constitutes an empirical attempt to analyse the antecedents of the reshoring strategy under current geopolitical instability. The narrative is based on multicriteria decision-making analysis and includes description of data collection techniques and expert involvement, thus reinforcing the study's rigour and enabling study replication in future. The study identifies a network of ten interrelated factors that influence the reshoring decisions of companies facing geopolitical turbulence. The modelling reveals which antecedents primarily drive relocation and trigger significant reactions among the other factors. The chapter also cross-references the study results with the existing debate on reshoring antecedents known from the literature.

Chapter 6, titled 'International production trajectories under geopolitical strain: The case of semiconductor and wire harness systems', presents an industry-specific analysis of a company's decision-making process in relocating its operations from China to an alternative location. The company, a manufacturer of wire harness systems, is highly dependent on the availability of semiconductors – a factor that significantly shapes its strategic choices. Faced with geopolitical uncertainty, the company evaluates various relocation options, including reshoring, nearshoring, and friendshoring. The study is conducted in collaboration with the company, comparing a data-driven, optimal site selection model with the firm's actual decision. This dual approach, combining statistical modelling with qualitative analysis, illustrates the practical value of the developed model in supporting corporate decision-making. Subsections of the chapter provide contextual background on the industry and assess alternative destination countries, considering factors identified in Chapter 5. The chapter also introduces a comparative analysis of Multicriteria Decision-Making methods, offering a systematic framework for evaluating and ranking location choices based on company's goals. Crucially, it incorporates managerial perspectives, shedding light on how executives navigate complex and uncertain environments and how subjective their decisions are. This real-world application strengthens the empirical value of the monograph.

Chapter 7 titled 'Policy frameworks for reshoring in CEE – review of the existing solutions and EU expectations' sets the previous analyses against the backdrop of the existing European reshoring framework. This chapter shifts the focus to a policy-level perspective, exploring how Central and Eastern European countries are responding to the reshoring trend. It begins by asking whether the EU has a coherent industrial policy or whether fragmented national strategies dominate. A critical discussion of whether a pan-European reshoring perspective exists, or whether countries are acting unilaterally, follows. The concluding goal is to become more self-reliant and resilient, particularly in key sectors, without turning to protectionism or isolationism. This chapter adds a governance dimension to the monograph, suggesting that firm-level decisions are increasingly influenced by regulatory regimes and adopted policies.

The final chapter synthesizes insights from across the monograph. It revisits the themes of geopolitical complexity, GVC reconfiguration, and policy evolution, tying them together into a cohesive narrative. The chapter outlines likely future research paths and suggests frameworks for further GVC resilience and adaptation.

In its structure, this monograph demonstrates a careful blend of conceptual approach empirical attempts to structure the relocation phenomenon and tie it to the existing policy frameworks. It navigates from macro-level geopolitics to firm-level decisions and policy implications, making it a valuable contribution to understanding how global production is evolving in a time of profound geopolitical uncertainty.

2 The three "de-"s

Global economy in face of geopolitical complexity

Numerous benefits of globalization, including higher economic growth, poverty reduction, and even lower inflation are often attributed to globalization (Garcia-Herrero, 2022). Yet, the rise of the "deglobalization" narrative is hard to overlook. Since 2020, this term has appeared in media over 4,500 times per year, with a surge to 7,323 references from January to November 2022 alone (Evenett, 2022). Even before that, Rodrik (2011) coined a term of "globalization paradox" where he stressed that it would be unlikely for globalization, democracy, and self-determination to coexist.

Recent geopolitical developments have contributed to the debate on (de)globalization. Studies on geopolitics and geoeconomics have shown that wars, terrorist attacks, and government interventions (Akadiri et al., 2020; Lu & Liu, 2024; Riti et al., 2022; Wernick, 2006) result in lower investment returns due to increased costs, which, in turn, discourage investors from further investments. Currently, many companies are re-evaluating their participation in global value chain (GVC) and some seek to relocate capital to countries with lower geopolitical risk (Abadie & Gardeazabal, 2003, 2008; Bandyopadhyay et al., 2014).

Geopolitics is associated with armed conflicts, political instability, and terrorist attacks, all of which have directly and indirectly influenced the development of investment patterns (Frey et al., 2007; Guo et al., 2023; Jensen, 2008; Li & Vashchilko, 2010). Investments in regions like Africa and the Middle East have long been affected by the aftermath of events such as the Arab Spring and the U.S. Peacekeeping Mission. Similarly, Brexit has had a lasting negative effect on investment in the UK (Mroczek-Dąbrowska & Jędrych-Matysek, 2022).

DOI: 10.4324/9781003724803-2

These examples represent just a fraction of the many geopolitical risks that must be factored into GVC reconfiguration. However, today, geopolitical risks no longer stem only from political instability, terrorism, and regional conflicts; they also encompass broader, unconventional threats, including cyber risks.

In this chapter, we explore the key geopolitical factors driving the deglobalization process between 2023 and 2025. We discuss trade and economic impact of geopolitical acts and threats. We then examine the origins and implementation of decoupling and de-risking strategies, along with their impact on the global economic power dynamics. The discussion then shifts to the interconnections between various end-game scenarios of deglobalization. The chapter strives to set the backdrop to later evaluate the GVCs' resilience strategies, companies can adopt to navigate the deglobalizing world.

The current geopolitical GVC risks

Any economic disruptions, instability, or negative outcomes stemming from political events or tensions between countries are referred to as geopolitical risk (GR). It has a broad meaning that includes "threat, realization, and escalation of adverse events associated with wars, terrorism, and any tensions among states and political actors that affect the peaceful course of international relations" (Caldara & Iacoviello, 2022, p. 1195). Based on this definition Caldara and Iacoviello developed an index of GR which analyses the frequency of mainstream media mentioning adverse geopolitical developments (Figure 2.1).

Not surprisingly, currently the GR index[1] is highest for countries experiencing armed conflicts (Ukraine, Israel). Additionally, the Authors differentiate between GR, "geopolitical acts" (GA) and "geopolitical threats" (GT). GA mean specific actions or behaviours undertaken by nations or political actors to trigger or escalate certain events while GT relate to threats and military buildups associated with potential conflict. The distinction emphasizes that it is not only the actual occurrence of a geopolitical development but the mere threat of such development that can have significant economic impact (Figure 2.2). The Geopolitical Risk (GPR) index at the end of 2025 has been significantly shaped by several key factors: military buildups, the onset and escalation of wars. In contrast, terror threats have consistently declined over the past decade. While the nuclear

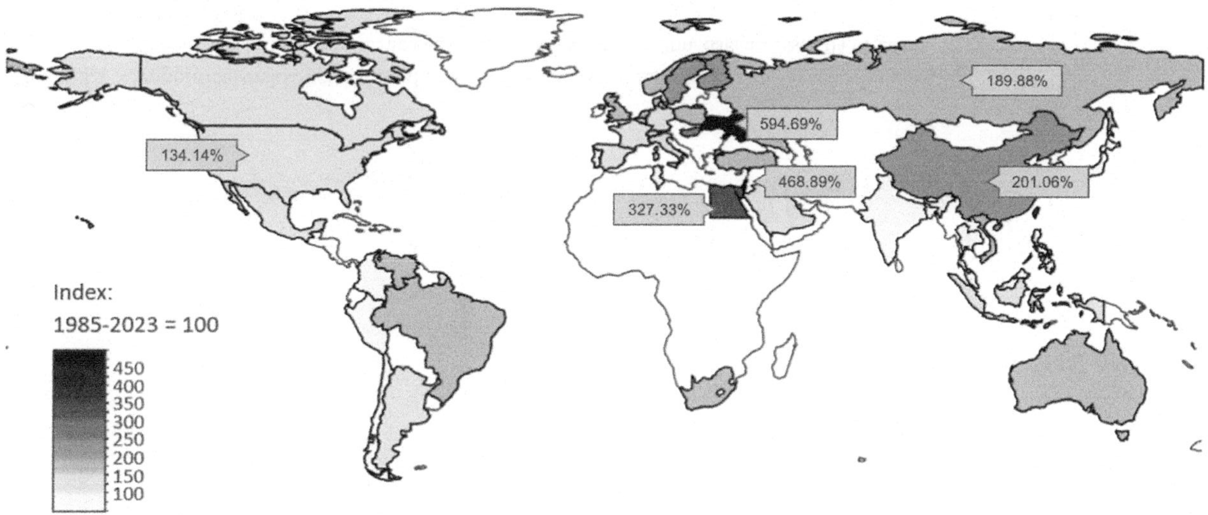

Figure 2.1 Geopolitical risk by country (state as of 2025).

Source: Own elaboration based on www.matteoiacoviello.com/gpr_country.htm, data accessed 04.02.2025.

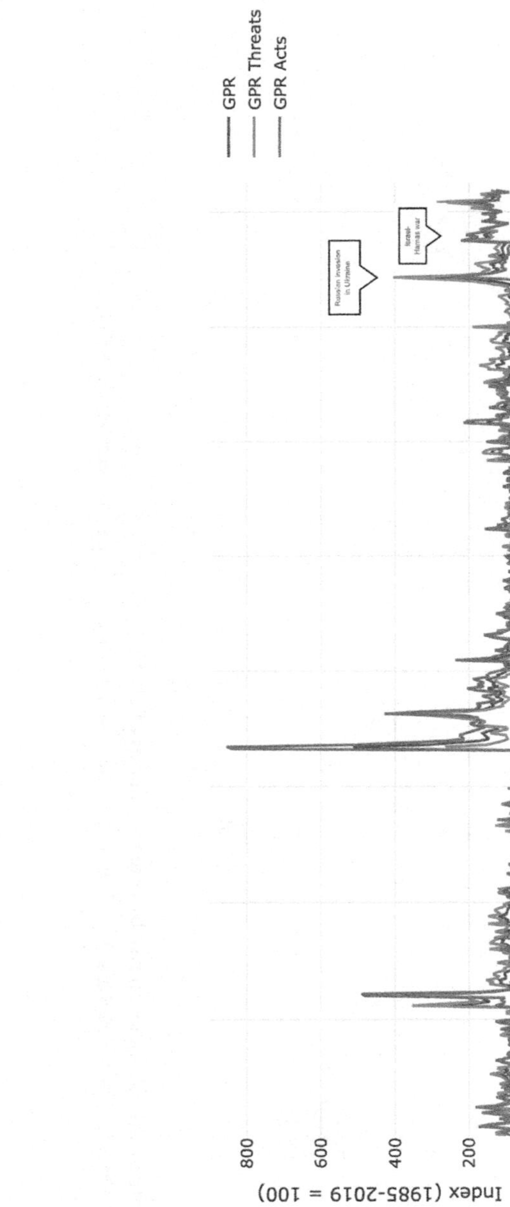

Figure 2.2 Geopolitical risks, geopolitical acts. and geopolitical threats.

Source: Own elaboration based on www.matteoiacoviello.com/gpr_country.htm, data accessed 04.02.2025.

threat has been increasing since 2022, it remains relatively low in the overall index.

The armed conflicts

Several armed conflicts today pose risks to global trade by disrupting shipments and supply chains. The most significant ones include the Russia–Ukraine war, the Israel-Hamas conflict, and ongoing tensions in the South China Sea. While some conflicts, like those in Africa, have more localized impacts, they still cause considerable disruptions to the flow of key resources.

The Russian invasion of Ukraine

Ukraine has been one of the largest exporters of grain, specifically of wheat, corn, and barley (Kacperska et al., 2025). Since February 2022, marking the Russian invasion in Ukraine, the trade in grain has been heavily impacted, as blockade of ports on the Black Sea disrupted shipments, leading to food shortages and price increases in regions dependent on Ukrainian supply, especially the Middle East, North Africa, and Asia. The situation was partially stabilized by the "Grain Agreement of 22 July 2022" signed by Ukraine, Russia, Türkiye, and the United Nations which ensured safe transportation through the Black Sea. However, challenges persisted, as Ukrainian ports continued to be attacked, insurance premium skyrocketed and the shipments remained at risk (Van Meijl et al., 2024). Russia terminated the agreement in July 2023, once again causing significant volatility in grain prices (Mohamad, 2024).

The European Union's (EU) response to Russia's invasion of Ukraine also had a major impact on the energy sector. Western sanctions and Russia's retaliatory actions caused short-term instability in the already volatile energy market. The EU Member States have been heavily reliant on the Russian energy and faced the threat of significant energy shortages and prices surge, which triggered a spike in inflation (Morão, 2025). In effect, countries have been diversifying energy sources, further disrupting long-standing trade routes and agreements. The Western countries, including the EU and the U.S. imposed a wide range of sanctions, expected to limit Russia's trade ability (De Souza et al., 2024). In effect, Russia pivoted toward

Asia, particularly in the gas and oil sectors (Lei & Sui, 2024; Pye et al., 2025) causing spatial shifts to global trade.

Moreover, both countries, Ukraine and Russia are key suppliers of metals, fertilizers, and certain raw materials. The invasion disrupted materials and components' availability creating bottlenecks in many GVCs, including electronics, construction, and agriculture. Significantly, the semiconductor industry has been hit hard. The war forced many countries to reevaluate their trade dependencies (see Chapter 7, specifically EU's Open Strategic Autonomy). It is expected that China will leverage the war, capitalizing on the GVCs' disruptions by securing more competitive prices for raw materials and energy. The Russia–Ukraine war has been *the* geopolitical trigger that caused both nations and businesses to rethink the future of globalization and the global order. It significantly disrupted the status quo and revealed underlying antagonism, giving China time and space to advance its interests in Taiwan and the South China Sea.

The Israel–Hamas conflict

The Gaza conflict dates back to 1948 but it has escalated in October 2023 with the Hamas's attack on Israel. The conflict has quickly evolved from a regional one to a threat of notable global ramifications. It continues to exert direct influence on waterway transportation routes (see the following subchapter on the Red Sea disturbance) but it has also impacted the regional trade (Bhattacharjee et al., 2024; Liu et al., 2024). Given Israel's prominent role as a major shipping hub, the escalation of the conflict has led to bottlenecks in port operations, logistics, and air traffic.

The regional trade between Israel and neighbouring countries experienced a severe setback. Türkiye has banned all trade with Israel as of mid-2024. In effect, the volume of bilateral trade between the countries dropped to $5.7 billion in 2023, compared to a record of $8 billion in 2022. Specifically, import of metals dropped more than tenfold, mineral products thirteenfold, chemicals eightfold, and plastic and rubber threefold.

The disrupted shipments

Since 2023, geopolitics-related disruptions emerged as a central concern for GVCs. The ongoing conflicts, such as the Russian invasion in Ukraine, the Israel-Hamas conflict, and the crisis in the Red Sea, have, following the COVID-19 pandemics, sent shockwaves through the supply chains, driving up shipping costs and disrupting the availability of critical materials and minerals.

The Red Sea is one of the key global interoceanic trade route with two main entry points: the Suez Canal in the north and the Bab al-Mandab Strait in the south. The Suez Canal alone handles nearly one-third of global container traffic and about 12–15% of global goods trade (Notteboom et al., 2024). The Israeli aggression in Gaza in November 2023 triggered the crisis when the Houthis joined the conflict to allegedly secure food and medicine pathways for Gaza (Bhagwat & Shaparov, 2024). In just half a year, between November 2023 and April 2024, 66 attacks on merchants ships were reported, causing a drastic spike in insurance rates and in consequence, making shipping companies opt for alternative routes, driving up both costs and lead times. The traffic through the Suez Canal dropped by 42% with vessels rerouting around the Cape of Good Hope. The lead times were extended by 20 to 24 days due to additional 4,000–6,000 nautical miles added through the detour. The cost of shipping a container to Europe has increased 5 times and the insurance premiums even 24 times (Townsend, 2024). The rerouting impacted also the environmental progress, as fuel consumption increased and added to the greenhouse gas emissions.

The global trade route has been affected, though there are some unconfirmed speculations[2] suggesting that Russia and China may have reached an agreement with the Houthis to ensure safe passage through the Red Sea. For China, this route has historically been crucial, with 80% of its exports to Europe passing through it, while for Russia, the route remains vital for transporting energy supplies to Asia (Bhagwat & Shaparov, 2024). The U.S. mediation attempts to stop the attacks on ships, including incentives like reopening Sana'a airport and Hodeidah port and providing government employees' compensation, were futile (Rodgers, 2024). In response, the U.S. formed a coalition against the Houthis, but it included far fewer countries than anticipated, with only 20 out of 42 Western and Arab nations officially joining. Belgium, France, Germany, Greece, Italy, and Sweden put forward their own overlapping operation, significantly diminishing the effect by uncoordinated actions. The rerouting has taken a heavy toll especially on the Indian shipping companies.

The Red Sea conflict resulted in distributions for the GVCs. Firstly, it impacted the fleet capacity. The usage of the Cape route led to "short-term capacity constraints, with a shortage of slot space for shippers" (Notteboom et al., 2024, p. 9). Likewise, the conflict resulted in short-term disruptions for the container business as many shipments were cancelled or rerouted, rendering some of the schedules unachievable. For now, using the Cape route has direct impact on the Mediterranean Basin, which was considered the "hub-of-hubs" linking four continents (Haralambides, 2023). Its accessibility is restricted to Straits of Gibraltar which may lead to redirecting the Europe–Asia shipments to Tanger Med, Algeciras, Sines, and Valencia, major northern European ports like Rotterdam, Hamburg, and Antwerp-Bruges or even West Africa.

Even though the Gaza ceasefire deal was signed in January 2025, the trade is yet not likely to return to the Red Sea, as companies are not convinced the attacks on merchandise ships will stop. In effect, alternative routes are being considered, as a permanent solution to the increasing geopolitical tensions. The India–Middle East–Europe Economic Corridor (IMEC) would enable transportation on both tangible and non-tangible goods, linking the Indian coast to European markets. The route includes waterway route from India to United Arab Emirates, followed by rail network to Saudi Arabia, Jordan, and Israel. Connection with Europe could be reached through Greece. However, the route also presents geopolitical challenges: it passes through waters disputed by Türkiye, involves Israel, which is part of the Gaza crisis, and requires substantial funding to build the necessary infrastructure. Since Türkiye opposes IMEC, it actively collaborates with Iraq, Qatar, and United Arab Emirates on the Iraq Development Road project, which will link the Gulf to Europe while bypassing Israel (Soylu, 2024). Additionally, Türkiye supports other projects that propose routes passing through its territory, including the Persian Pipeline, the Trans-Caspian Pipeline, the Qatar-Türkiye Pipeline, and the Southern Gas Corridor. Russia–Asia trade is likely to follow The International North-South Transport Corridor (INSTC) which, unlike IMEC, is already in use. The route is also being used for shipping the goods from China to Europe and the transit is said to be about 20 days shorter than through Suez Canal (Bhagwat & Shaparov, 2024).

Sanctions, countersanctions, and trade weaponization

The rise of protectionism and geopolitical uncertainty has led to an increased use of economic sanctions, especially following the

Russia–Ukraine conflict, U.S.–China tech tensions and Iranian conflict. The sanctions imposed go far beyond individuals or companies and have started to target whole industries creating sudden, wide-reaching trade disruptions. The distribution of the sanctions is not even, with advanced economies often prevailing as sanction's initiator while the emerging economies are their main target (Cipollina & Dal Bianco, 2025). Recent data on sanctions suggest a more nuanced picture, indicating that sanctions are not exclusively directed at developing countries; major global powers are also increasingly subject to their impact (Figure 2.3).

Following Russia's invasion in Ukraine, sanctions have re-emerged at the forefront of international attention. For instance, Canada, Japan, and the UK imposed import tariffs on Russian goods, ranging from 8% to 35%. Western countries collectively revoked Russia's "Most Favored Nation" (MFN) status, thereby granting themselves the legal latitude to impose discretionary tariffs without violating World Trade Organization rules. Simultaneously political leaders have advocated for embargoes on Russian oil and gas imports (De Souza et al., 2024). Similar measures were also extended towards Belarus.

The economic effectiveness of sanctions is, however, limited, and a vast number of researchers focus on delineating how sanctions should be used to ultimately minimize the cost for the sanctioning countries (Becko, 2024). Sanctions, however, are also a flagship tool for exerting political pressure rather than achieving specific economic gains (cf. Kim et al., 2023). Therefore, they remain a key instrument within the geopolitical landscape, closely related to the current threats present in global geopolitics.

Election campaign pledges and protectionism

During the U.S. presidential election campaign, Donald Trump promised to raise tariff barriers in an effort to boost domestic job growth. Between 1990 and 2007, during the offshoring trend, it's estimated that the U.S. lost around 21% of its manufacturing jobs, totalling 1.53 million positions to China alone. The pledge was driven by a populist desire to revive the Rust Belt,[3] a once-thriving industrial region. In his campaign, Donald Trump suggested a 10% across-the-board tariff on all trading partners and 60% or higher tariffs on Chinese goods (Clausing & Obstfeld, 2024). Simultaneously, he proposed cutting income taxes – potentially by up to $5 trillion over a

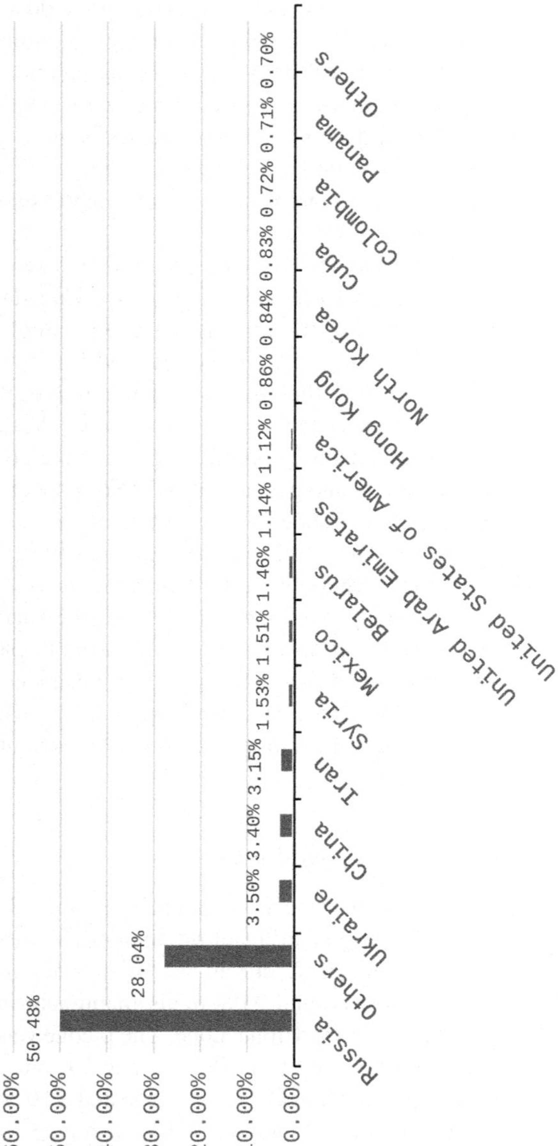

Figure 2.3 Share of sanctioned entities per country (as of June 2025).
Source: Own elaboration based on OpenSanctions database (accessed 19.06.2025).

decade – and has floated the idea of replacing income taxes with tariff revenue. Imposing a 60% tariff on Chinese imports largely achieves the goal of creating manufacturing jobs, but not without significant losses for households when adjusted for inflation. Likewise, tariff revenue would not fully replace income tax revenue as imports (estimated at $3.1 trillion in 2023) are a much smaller tax base compared to income (estimated at $20+ trillion).

The tariff threats could also provoke retaliation from trading partners, harming global trade, growth, and cooperation, not only in business, but on general issues like climate change and security. Higher tariffs could cause the U.S. dollar to appreciate, worsening trade deficits and creating financial instability for countries with dollar-denominated debt. Since many manufacturing companies rely on foreign parts and components, raising tariffs on all U.S. imports does not lead to additional jobs, but it does further increase the cost of living, reducing competitiveness and economic efficiency. According to Evenett and Muendler (2025), projections on employment changes in the U.S. suggest that only the proposed 60% tariff on Chinese goods would lead to a meaningful increase in jobs. In contrast, a 25% ad valorem tariff on imports from Mexico and Canada would have minimal impact, while tariffs on other countries would ultimately backfire, leading to job losses rather than employment gains in the U.S.

For the EU, the short-term impact of Trump's 2.0 tariffs is expected to be negative, leading to a decline in exports to the U.S. In 2023, the EU exported €502 billion in goods and €292 billion in services to the U.S. (Stamer, 2024). However, economic models suggest that these negative effects would fade within one to two years. Even if China retaliates with a 60% tariff and other nations impose 10% tariffs on U.S. goods, the impact on Europe's economy would remain limited. This is because U.S. imports are not a major factor for Europe, and retaliatory tariffs on U.S. goods would actually boost European competitiveness in global markets. An interesting study by Bouët et al. (2024) reveals that by 2030 the 10–60% scenario could actually strengthen the bilateral trade flows between Canada, Mexico, and U.S., while significantly reducing economic dependence on China. Meanwhile, China–EU trade flows are expected to see moderate growth, positioning China as a net exporter within these shifting trade dynamics. Ultimately, these changes would lead to a more regionalized global trade system.

The ongoing tariff debacle has significantly increased trade uncertainty (Piserà et al., 2025). Since April 2025, the Trump's administration has repeatedly announced, suspended, renegotiated, and reintroduced a number of tariffs and other trade barriers targeting both various products and countries. These range from 10% up to 50%, on average (Wengerek et al., 2025). The measures applied appear inconsistent, quite unpredictable, and seem to be lacking a coherent policy rationale. Additionally, the announced conditions for their withdrawal do not correspond with real economic issues and, even if they are met, the tariff retreatment is not realized which has the trade partners questioning the administration's real intentions. Furthermore, the EU has been publicly accused of having been formed to undermine the U.S.'s economic status; a claim used to justify the imposition of various trade barriers. For instance, U.S. tariffs on steel and aluminium have reached 25% and can be potentially even doubled in the forthcoming months. Similar protectionist actions were directed at the automotive industry and other crucial trade areas. In response, the EU prepared and announced its own countermeasures, currently valued at ca. €96 billion, which may lead to a serious escalation in trade tensions.

This tit-for-tat dynamic between the U.S. and their trade partners created a protracted and exhaustive negotiation cycle, on one hand designed at reestablishing a degree of mutual agreement to mitigate the economic fallout but on the other, only adding to the existing global uncertainty. While specific tariff rates continue to fluctuate, the broader geoeconomic strategy of the U.S. is becoming increasingly evident. The U.S. aims at preserving (or reclaiming) their global economic dominance through aggressive, unilateral measures. However, this approach carries significant risks. Ultimately, at least short-term, it may prove counterproductive since trust in the U.S. is undermined and retaliatory actions are undertaken. Trade partners are excluding the U.S. from some of their bi- and multi-lateral agreements, eroding the "Western" economic block's position within the global economic system (cf. Contractor, 2025).

Institutional weakness under geopolitical duress

There are several international institutions that regulate the global trade, including the World Trade Organization (WTO), International Monetary Fund (IMF), World Bank (WB), United Nations Conference on Trade and Development (UNCTAD), Organisation for Economic Co-operation and Development (OECD), and others. WTO, established in 1995, has played a crucial role in facilitating global trade by setting rules, resolving disputes, and promoting trade liberalization. Yet, the last decade has revealed its structural challenges that have undermined its effectiveness, leading to concerns about its relevance and legitimacy (Bunel et al., 2022).

Recently, one of the WTO's discussed weaknesses is its consensus-based decision-making process. Unlike some other international organizations that use weighted voting, the WTO must secure agreement among all 164 members to reach a decision[4] (Low, 2011). In effect, the system hinders responsiveness, making it difficult to adapt to new global challenges, which was well proven by the COVID-19 pandemics (Pushp et al., 2024). Likewise, trade liberalization efforts, especially in services, can be easily diluted or blocked, leading to an increase in bilateral and regional trade agreements that bypass the WTO, further questioning its very relevance. Moreover, the WTO's dispute settlement system, once regarded as its strongest pillar, has been effectively paralyzed and non-functional since 2019 when the U.S. started blocking appointments to the Appellate Body. Until then, the settlement of disputes in the WTO functioned quite well as the procedures were rules-based, automatic, and prompt (Kaushik, 2024). For example, in its 30 years, the WTO has ruled on 629 disputes, whereas its predecessor, General Agreement on Tariffs and Trade (GATT), handled only 316 cases over nearly 50 years. However, the U.S. claims that the Appellate Body has overstepped and has been engaging in what they call the "judicial activism". As a result, nowadays approximately 30 disputes remain unresolved, allowing some countries to take unilateral trade actions without legal repercussions. In effect, countries including China, the EU, and Canada have turned to alternative mechanisms such as the Multi-Party Interim Appeal Arbitration Arrangement (MPIA), which excludes the U.S., further diminishing the WTO's authority (Pahis, 2024).

While the blockage of the Appellate Body is often attributed to it exceeding its mandate, it is also closely tied to issues involving China. China's economic model is non-market oriented, relying heavily on government subsidies. It strongly supports its many state-owned firms and enforces technology transfers, all of which contribute to trade distortions (Hopewell, 2025; Qianyi, 2025). WTO seems unable to address China's economic policies, including the U.S.–China tariff conflict, further deepening the Appellate Body deadlock. Furthermore, under the WTO's self-declaration mechanism, China remains classified as a developing country which grants it certain trade benefits such as longer implementation timelines and special market access provisions (Yap, 2024). This is yet another bone of contention amid the geopolitical and geoeconomic powerplay between the U.S. and China. In fact, the self-determination casts doubt on the "developing" status of several other countries, like India, Singapore, Israel, Mexico, Türkiye, Chile, Indonesia, South Africa, South Korea, the United Arab Emirates or Qatar (Bunel et al., 2022). Lack of clear criteria for the "developing" country status results in growing resistance of developed countries to grant any trade concessions in bilateral agreements, further weakening the WTO's mandate. In effect, not only the Appellate Body is being bypassed. In negotiating trade agreements, countries have increasingly turned to regional and plurilateral agreements, such as the Trans-Pacific Partnership (TPP) and the Regional Comprehensive Economic Partnership (RCEP), which operate outside the WTO's framework (Kong et al., 2025; Rimmer, 2024).

WTO is facing geopolitics-related challenges not only due to the U.S.–China tensions but also because of other geopolitical conflicts. The Russian invasion in Ukraine in February 2022 led to implementation of trade sanctions on Russia and Belarus, particularly by the Western countries. The sanctions targeted the main trade flows, including finance, energy and defence sectors (Taira, 2024). Whilst WTO generally upholds the principles of free trade, it now struggles to reconcile the non-discriminatory commitment with the heated power struggle (Kawashima, 2024). Ukraine-supporting countries also sought to leverage WTO and sanction Russia for violation of international law. While WTO does not hold a mandate to expel members, Russia's participation in certain WTO activities (especially regarding dispute resolution) was suspended and some of the trade privileges were revoked. Although WTO as an organization maintains neutral stance in geopolitical disputes, it has been urged to directly address the conflict as it caused trade disruptions, particularly in Europe and Africa. Although the invasion started in 2022, it continues to challenge the WTO's traditional approach to trade governance based on multilateralism. Likewise, other geopolitical disputes, including Trump's potential trade tariffs, the India–U.S. conflict over agricultural subsidies, South China Sea tensions or Middle East Tensions, are expected to fuel the debate on WTO's future role in trade. The increasing intersection of geopolitics and trade points to a fragmentation of global trade into blocs, prompting a reconsideration of the WTO's governance approach.

Deglobalization, decoupling, and de-risking – towards a multipolar global economy?

Deglobalization is commonly and unanimously understood as "the process of weakening interdependence among nations" (Witt, 2019, p. 1054). A retrospective study allows us to conclude that we have already entered the deglobalization stage. Global trade peaked between 2007 and 2010 whilst foreign direct investment (FDI) continued to grow till 2011, later triggering a moderate yet persistent decline. The data on FDI inflows suggests a more profound decline than the one observed in case of imports of goods and services (Witt, 2019). Although the exact anchor point marking deglobalization is debatable with numerous studies (Dreher, 2006; Gygli et al., 2018) investigating Konjunkturforschungsstelle (KOF) Globalization index, investment restrictions or regulatory changes, the fact remains that downward trends among all outputs are observable. Yet, since deglobalization is a process and not an outcome international presence and activities will not cease to exist (completely deglobalized economy, autarky) but lead to lessening of the international interdependencies (Witt et al., 2023).

The genesis of deglobalization, including its drivers, has been widely studied (Cuervo-Cazurra et al., 2020; Kobrin, 2017; Witt, 2019) and points to political and geopolitical factors as one of the key determinants fuelling the process. Witt (2019) advocates that both liberalism and realism are relevant political science theories that contribute to explaining the phenomenon. Liberalists argue that globalization is determined by states' agreement to cooperate (for mutual benefit) and establishing international institutions (also known as international regimes). Deglobalization occurs if the developed institutional infrastructure meant to support globalization fails (e.g. the Doha round of WTO negotiations, WTO Appellate Body crisis) which in turn impacts the openness for economic cooperation. Secondly the cooperation payoff also changes in time, significantly altering the willingness to uphold it (Buckley, 2023). The examples from past years are in abundance: the European migration crisis, Brexit, Sino–U.S. trade war and many other occurrences have empowered the globalization critics to question the long-term gains distributions and impact. Likewise, realists seek to explain deglobalization through the concept of hegemonic stability theory (Krasner, 1976). In this perspective a hegemon understood as a state exerting dominant influence on other states, is normally able to establish and force upon others an international institutional regime that benefits mostly the hegemon. Once the hegemon's relative power subsides, the deglobalization begins (Witt, 2019; Witt et al., 2023). Hence, the hegemonic stability theory claims that global cooperation is underpinned by influence and leadership of the world's most powerful country which in the past years has been the United States of America (U.S.). Currently, a dominant thought prevails that the world lacks a hegemon. The U.S. has lost its position both in relation to economic and military power. China has yet to ascend to that place, prevailing mostly regionally and still not globally.

Both theories contribute to the discussion on how the global economy will continue to function in the deglobalization era. The liberal approach advocates for the emergence of patchwork system, a number of bilateral or regional trade agreements based on individual interests and securing varying level of interdependencies (Aggarwal & Urata, 2006; Shadlen, 2008). An extreme outcome could include the existence of trade and economic blocks with high inter-block restrictions. The realism perspective implies various pathways: emergence of a new hegemon, multipolarism, and disorder. With U.S. losing its hegemony and China not yet reaching it, the discussion also implies that India might be considered as viable candidate whilst EU definitely not (Webber, 2016). Although EU is considered "big enough" for the status, its near-consensual decision-making process and increasingly self-serving attitude of member states deem the superpower position unreachable. The multipolar outcome resembles the patchwork system with at least two (if not more) regional hegemons emerging. The disorder is less likely to appear but would mean significant destabilization of the existing status quo with no structured alternative to succeed it.

As a consequence, a new phenomenon has appeared which nowadays is broadly discussed – the decoupling process. Decoupling refers directly to the deglobalization but whereas deglobalization meant weakening interdependence among nations, decoupling refers to weakening interdependence between specific states or blocks (Witt et al., 2023). Contemporary studies focus on the Sino–U.S. decoupling that will now be supplemented by the context of Russian invasion in Ukraine and further geopolitical polarization (Tung et al., 2023; Witt et al., 2023; Yang & Chan, 2023). The Sino–U.S. bifurcation is attributed to the China's swift ascendancy that threatened the existing status quo. Trump's administration triggered the so-called trade war by imposing tariffs and thus initiating a series of tit-for-tat countersanctions (Casson, 2021; Luo, 2022; Luo & Van Assche, 2023). The antagonism is now being strengthened by China's continuous support for Russia, both economic through import of coal and oil as well as political by China refusing to condemn the Russian invasion in United Nations forum. Additionally, China introduced a series of policy initiatives including "Made in China 2025" and "The Belt and Road Initiative" that are meant to ensure China's technological self-reliance but at the same time safeguard China's position as key supplier of technological solutions hence leveraging its position in the GVCs over its trade partners. The U.S. countered these initiatives by the "Chip 4 Alliance", an agreement between U.S., Japan, Taiwan, and South Korea on cooperation in manufacturing chips. This rivalry led to what we call techno-nationalism, a geopolitical strain linking state's technological capabilities with national security (Luo, 2022). Yet, although China and U.S. remain in the spotlight, their decoupling process directly affects other economies, especially through FDI flow shifts.

Decoupling has led to the implementation of de-risking strategies among many companies. For instance, many of the European manufacturers, including Spanish, Italian, and German companies dependent on the Chinese exports have either adopted dual sourcing strategies or tuned to European suppliers altogether (Di Stefano et al., 2022). Other changes include shifts in GVCs. Under the concept of Global Factory, multinational enterprises (MNEs) their operations were "sliced" and certain stages of activities were located in chosen location which enabled the companies to control the value chain without necessarily owning it all (Buckley, 2011). However, the concept took economic openness for granted and deglobalization now will likely create new transactional costs stemming from unpredictable institutional arbitrage. What is expected is that China might attempt to enforce new institutional norms that would succeed the receding Western framework and significantly add to GVC risk levels. In effect, we may expect that reshoring and friendshoring practices to gain on momentum. Simplifying the issue, reshoring is understood as bringing the activities back to the home country while friendshoring refers to keeping them offshored but relocating them to a country aligned with the home country (especially in political perspective) (Dachs et al., 2019; Gray et al., 2013). The scale of these trends is dependable on reshorability of the processes, i.e. the access to the resources (labour, materials, etc.) needed for the manufacturing and strategic importance, i.e. perception of the importance of the product (or service) to the home national security (Witt et al., 2023). If the strategic importance is assessed as high and the reshorability similarly, then we expect to encounter reshoring tendencies. If however, reshorability is low, relocating in form of friendshoring is more probable. Yet, should the strategic importance be perceived as low any of the options is feasible, including staying in the initially offshored location. To aid these trends we observe a resurge of the previously strongly criticized industrial policy. The Chip Act of 2022 is just one of the flagship examples of such attempts.

The EU is increasingly eager to proactively mitigate reliance on China which has not proven easy. This is evidenced by distinct developments but significantly, for the first time, the outflow of FDI from China has exceeded the inflow. Yet still China dominates in the supply of raw materials, especially those needed in the manufacturing process of high-tech components and products. Certain dependencies in the GVCs are irreplaceable or extremely difficult to substitute, granting significant influence to China. For instance, China has imposed export restrictions on crucial semiconductor materials such as germanium, gallium, and graphite. These elements are essential in manufacturing a wide array of products, including semiconductors, LEDs, solar panels, microprocessors, and solar cells, as well as in military technologies like night vision goggles (Harvén, 2023). A remedy for the Chinese dominance is sought in circular economy where it is estimated that European companies could reduce their critical material dependence by 70% if they turned to recycling and increased their mining and processing capacity. Simultaneously, EU is planning to leverage its position by restricting the flow of critical technologies to China. EU policy makers target especially those companies that continue exporting to Russia for both civilian and military purposes. China is believed to be sidestepping sanctions, convinced that no counteractions are forthcoming due to Europe's reliance on the country.

The EU's de-risking attempts are aimed at re-establishing its geoeconomic[5] position. In 2023 the European Commission endorsed a de-risking strategy that addressed challenges arising from GVCs' disruptions, economic coercion, unintended technology leakage, as well as critical infrastructure disruptions (Gehrke & Medunic, 2024). Yet, the proposed agenda is still narrow, passive, and defensive, based on "promoting" and expecting "partnerships" to ensure economic security. It also lacks clear vision on addressing trade-offs between reaching geoeconomic goals and other aims, such as greening the GVCs. Establishing a geoeconomic strategy requires EU to proactively leverage its strengths to re-establish the block's position in the global economy. In the past EU adopted a proactive approach by setting standards in green and digital transformation of supply chains. It has however failed to become the standard-maker for its geostrategic purposes. The U.S.' agenda is set about winning the technological and economic race with China. China on the other hand aims to de-risk by ensuring national control over parts of global economy. Although the geostrategies are different, they are certainly proactive and are not limited to mitigation of the existing risk but are already considering potential future disruptions. For Europe, it is expected that three main factors will be key to establishing a sound geostrategy; these factors are China, the U.S., and Russia.

Geopolitical alignment, trade, and investment

The geopolitical alignment indicates that countries tend to associate with those partners that share their interests, values, and security concerns. This alignment can be economic, political, and military in nature (Bhaumik et al., 2025). Historically, in the post-World War II world, the choice of alignment was between the U.S. and the Soviet Union and even the countries that belonged to the so-called non-alignment movement (NAM) often ended up siding with one of the superpowers on one occasion or the other. After the Cold War, these relationships became more complex with the emergence to power of countries like China, India, Brazil, and Russia. While not global hegemons, their growing influence significantly reshaped the geopolitical landscape.

The rational for the choice of geopolitical alignment is still debated. On one hand, Wendt (1992) claims that it is driven by shared norms and values, pointing to political similarity as a basis for alliance formation. Here, the U.S. and Western Europe are cited as examples where a shared commitment to democracy reinforces their bond. Yet, recently scholars point also to shared interest in shaping alignment. This evolving perspective, known as the "balance-of-beliefs" approach, suggests that pursuing common goals can be just as effective in alliance formation as ideological alignment. An adequate example would be the relationship between Russia and China, which is driven largely by their mutual aim to counterbalance and reduce U.S. dominance (Feng & He, 2024).

Literature suggests that geopolitical alignment directly translates to bilateral aid and access to lending (Faye & Niehaus, 2012). It is also associated with greater FDI flows and trade flows although the impact of the latter appears to be gradually declining (Bhaumik et al., 2025; Jakubik & Ruta, 2023). Aiyar et al. (2024) studied the alignment of FDI flows with the geopolitical alliance formation over the last 20 years. Their study revealed that the flows are becoming increasingly concentrated among geopolitically aligned countries, particularly in strategic sectors. The probability of an investment being made between aligned countries is more than twice as high as between non-aligned countries. This probability is even higher (2.5 times) in the recent years given the increasing uncertainty and geopolitical disruptions. In effect, the geoeconomic fragmentation will likely lead to overall global output losses with the low-income countries and emerging markets taking the highest toll. We could expect that some collective efforts to mitigate global risks (e.g. environmental aim) will be taken on multilateral level but other areas where national interest prevail can experience setbacks.

Notes

1 The peak of the index (GPR>850) was reported for September 2001 after 9/11. The data is collected via American resources and although the general overview remains valid, the perspective is reflected in the GPR scores.

2 The speculations stem from the pattern of attacks, with Russian ships having been targeted only twice. The second attempt was attributed to the vessel being linked to the United Kingdom.

3 Rust Belt includes parts of states like Pennsylvania, Ohio, Michigan, Indiana, and Illinois and refers to an area that has experienced economic decline, with factories closing down or relocating to other countries, due to globalization, automation, and a shift towards a more service-based economy.

4 Consensus does not mean unanimity but rather that no member formally objects to the decision.

5 Geoeconomics and geopolitics are two interconnected terms. Geoeconomics is often referred to as a subset of geopolitics, focusing on economic rather than military or diplomatic power. The aim of the geoeconomic strategy would be to attain and preserve a privileged position in the globalized economy (Csurgai, 2017).

3 Global value chains and megatrends

The global value chain paradigm?

Global value chain (GVC) paradigm refers to how production processes are organized across various countries, with subsequent stages of production being outsourced or offshored to certain locations. The paradigm focuses on how and where the value is created, starting from the sourcing of raw materials up to the final product launched in the markets. The GVC framework assumes that global economic integration should lead to increased efficiency and thus, the economic growth. It also highlights the interdependence of firms, industries, and states. In practice, GVCs are often interchangeably labelled global production networks (GPN) or global commodity chains (GCC), although GVCs have a broader focus that goes beyond just trade and commodities. While all three frameworks explore the globalization of production, GVC focuses on the value-added aspects, GCC on flow of commodities and trade (Ponte, 2002), and GPN on the relationships and networks between firms (Coe et al., 2008). Yet, numerous papers relating to the three concepts often cover overlapping issues, indicating that the borders among the terms remain blurry and the frameworks themselves are interdisciplinary.

The development of the GVC concept was not a linear one (Inomata, 2017). The origins can be traced back to the neoclassical theory of international trade, where markets were considered as perfectly competitive, producers were homogenous, and countries were expected to trade in final goods only. With time, we observed a paradigm shift with works on intra-industry trade (Grubel & Lloyd, 1971), new trade theory (Helpman & Krugman, 1985), relocation and industry productivity (Melitz, 2003) leading to the understanding that

DOI: 10.4324/9781003724803-3

heterogenous producers operate on an increasing returns to scale and trade in tasks not final goods (Figure 3.1). This marked a critical step toward understanding fragmented production.

The term of value chain itself originates in business management studies and was coined by Porter (1985). It can be defined as set of activities that follow one another and are interdependent to collectively fulfil business goals. The GVCs in a way refer to the value chain concept however the activities are not contained within a company, but the company seeks to optimize the operations by potentially transferring them outside the firm. Baldwin (2013) in his historical perspective on unbundling discusses the events that led to the development of GVCs. If we consider three types of costs: shipping costs, communication costs, and face-to-face interaction costs we encounter two unbundling phases where we observe an increase in relocation of firms' activities. The first unbundling is associated with the sharp drop in transportation costs (steam revolution) and the second with

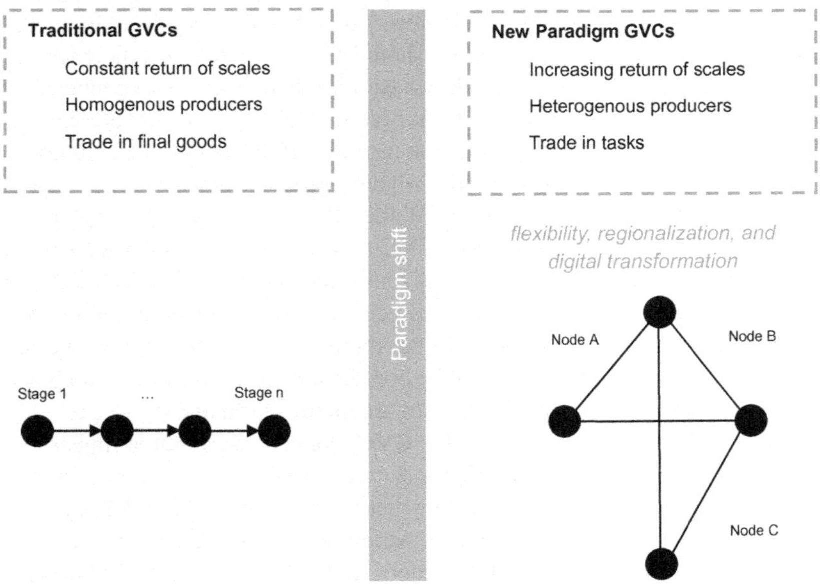

Figure 3.1 Paradigm shift in GVC studies.
Source: Own elaboration.

the drop in communication costs (ICT revolution). Along the second unbundling, segmentation and fragmentation became possible leading companies to (possibly) engage in vertical integration. Here, the transaction costs theory became the prominent framework to discuss the preferred mode of organizing the value chains.

In effect, Gereffi, Humphrey, and Sturgeon (2005) suggested a GVC typology based on three criteria: complexity of transactions, ability to codify transactions, and capabilities in the supply base. They referred to the global commodity chains by analyzing power relations and coordination mechanisms among lead firms and suppliers. Their "five governance types" – market, modular, relational, captive, and hierarchy – remain central to GVC analysis. The market-type GVC assumes little power asymmetry, meaning that both the supplier and the client can easily switch partners with minimal transaction costs. Transactions are market-based and are in constant flux. The modular-type GVC is quite similar with the exception of perception of the transactions' complexity. This may lead to an increase of transaction costs when changing partners but they still remain relatively low. The relational-type GVC describe an arrangement where both parties are mutually dependent. Transactions tend to be asset-specific and switching costs increase significantly. Captive-type was used in cases of extreme power asymmetry. This was prominent with major industry players and their small subcontractors or suppliers. Here, the dependence is one-sided as are the partner switching costs. Finally, the hierarchy-type GVC was specific to cases where the arrangements were kept within a corporate group, and we have observed vertical integration.

On empirical level, economic modelling evolved to address GVC geographical configuration, for instance the offshoring phenomenon and its impact on wages and welfare (Feenstra & Hanson, 1996) and trade in tasks (Grossman & Rossi-Hansberg, 2008). These models examined how relocating tasks affects productivity, labour demand, and income distribution. Contract theory (Grossman & Hart, 1986) and property-rights approaches (Antras, 2003) linked organizational choices – make-or-buy decisions – to incomplete contracts and firm heterogeneity. Later, Antràs & Chor (2013) introduced sequentiality, showing governance varies along production stages depending on complementarities or substitutability. Micro-level empirical research followed, initially using firm-level case studies and later multicountry input–output tables to measure trade in value added

(Johnson & Noguera, 2012). These methods revealed that gross trade statistics overstate bilateral imbalances and obscure the true origin of value creation. Advanced metrics now capture vertical specialization, supply chain length, and upstreamness, offering insights into fragmentation and positioning within GVCs.

Initially, the research related to GVCs focused on the value creation along the production chains, strongly emphasizing the role the governance structures played in shaping the power struggle between firms and their suppliers. With time, the attention shifted toward the GVC location patterns and its impact on emerging economies, as well as the role institutions played in GVC rollout. Yet, as could have been expected, the paradigm has undergone further changes triggered by the recent disruptions – including the COVID-19 pandemic, U.S.–China trade tensions, and war-related energy shocks, that exposed the fragility of the supply networks. In effect, scholars and policymakers are now questioning the once-dominant logic of offshoring that was underlying the GVC paradigm and are now discussing how autonomy and regionalization fit the creation of resilient GVC. Contemporary, the studies on GVC incorporate considerations including environmental sustainability, labour rights, and technological sovereignty which shifts our understanding of GVCs the previous purely economic framework to a more multidimensional one (Park, 2023). This shift marks a transition on how GVCs are viewed nowadays, as a dynamic system exposed to global shocks, adaptable to state interventions and shifting corporate strategies (Figure 3.2).

The GVC paradigm is inherently interdisciplinary, combining economics, sociology, and management. The concept of GVCs evolved leading to new research avenues. Its themes extend beyond trade theory to issues of industrial upgrading, innovation spillovers, labour market polarization, and policy design for development. In today's world of geopolitical tensions and technological disruptions, understanding GVCs is vital for crafting resilient and inclusive global production systems. On one hand, we have observed attempts to empirically measure various aspects of GVCs, including the production fragmentation, impact of relocation strategies on welfare, and GVCs governance modes. On the other hand, the GVC framework intertwined with a variety of social elements, making the concept an interdisciplinary term. Contemporary, GVC literature includes studies on: industry transformation process, labour market, regional development, digital spillovers, economic crisis, organizational resilience, sustainability

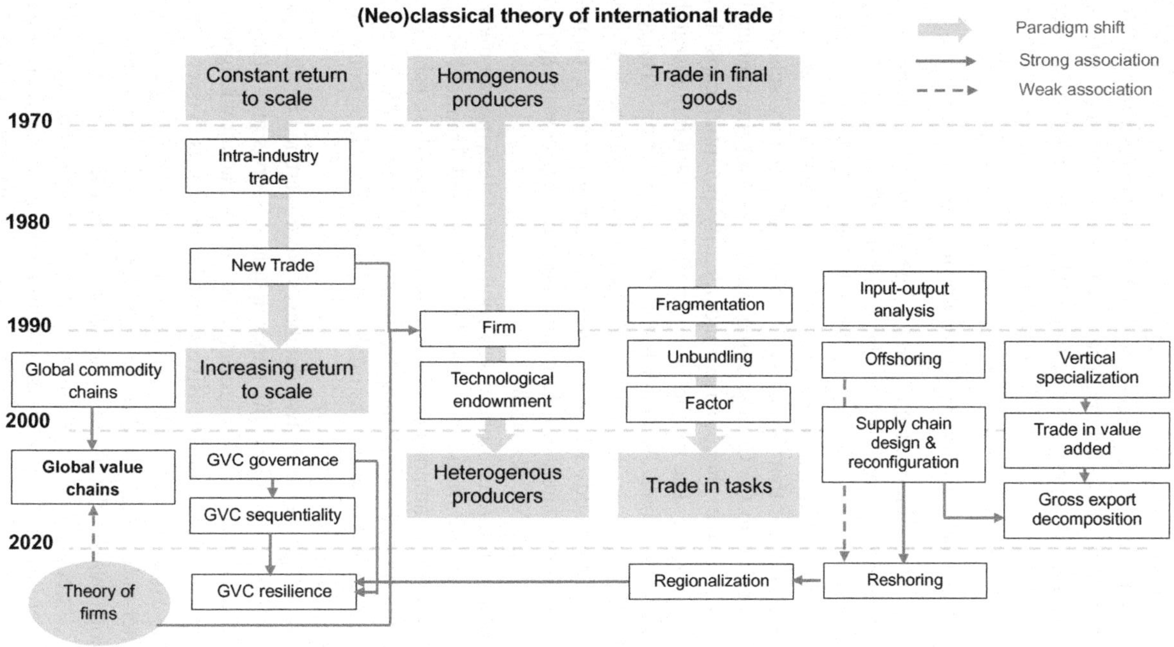

Figure 3.2 Analytical frameworks for global value chains – dependency map.

Source: Own elaboration based on (Inomata, 2017).

and climate change, consumer protection, poverty alleviation, trade arrangements, and national accounts (Inomata, 2017). The following section intends to verify, with use of systematic literature review, what potential research gaps and directions can be found in relation to GVC and the commonly discussed megatrends. As mentioned in Chapter 1, we find ourselves in highly volatile times which are expected to exert impact on the way in which GVCs operate.

Toward an understanding of the GVC megatrends

Even though the three megatrends – geopolitics, sustainability, and digitalization – contribute to the rewiring of the GVCs as we have known them, there is limited knowledge on how these three perspectives intertwine. Hence, it is crucial to conduct a systematic literature review that would synthesize contemporary scholarly work in reference to GVCs. By doing so, we expand the scholarly understanding of the phenomenon and identify potential gaps that still need addressing. The synthesis might aid unite different research streams and contribute to interdisciplinary integration (Burgers et al., 2019). Moreover, the review allows for mapping the linkages between the megatrends which in times of high uncertainty, unpredictability, and abundancy of information becomes a necessary step in progressing in the GVC research.

A systematic literature review was conducted following the methodology outlined by Mariano and Laker (2024) and Tranfield et al. (2003). The review intended to identify, select, and analyse scholarly contributions on GVCs and megatrends and summarize the results. A structured review process was established including three consecutive phases (Table 3.1).

In phase one of the study two databases were searched to identify, select, and further download the paper details – Scopus and Elsevier (ScienceDirect). These two sources are commonly acknowledged as the most reliable and comprehensive scientific databases (Visser et al., 2021). Keywords were established based on the usage of thesaurus in computer-aided search and retrieval processes.[1] They included the term "Global value chain" and one of the three megatrends "digitalization", "geopolitics", or "sustainability". British and American spelling were applied as were any commonly used abbreviations. Additionally, the search was limited to journal papers in English, related to fields of "Business, Management and Accounting" or

Table 3.1 Systematic literature review protocol

Phase 1: Identification, selection, and retrieval of dataset		
Step 1	– Scopus and Elsevier (ScienceDirect) database search per identified keywords: "Global value chain and geopolitics" OR "Global value chain and digitalization" OR "Global value chain and sustainability" (both British and American spelling used), – No specified timeframe, – Limited to: "Business, Management and Accounting" OR "Economics, Econometrics and Finance", – Language: English	N=970
Step 2	– Exclusion of duplicates, not peer-reviewed papers, editorials, viewpoints, conference papers, books, book chapters, and book reviews	N=639
Step 3	– General overview of keywords, overlay, and linkages	N=639
Phase 2: Retrieving, organization, and analysis of material		
Step 1	– Limitation of the papers to overlying items "Global value chain and geopolitics and digitalisation and sustainability" keywords – Download of peer-reviewed articles from Scopus and Elsevier (ScienceDirect) databases, and subsequent upload in a Zotero software	N=12
Step 2	– Analysis of the peer-reviewed papers: author(s), title, source, type of paper (i.e., conceptual, empirical), methodology (i.e. quantitative, qualitative, mixed), level of analysis, theories employed, key findings, and future research directions per each article	N=12
Phase 3: Synthesis and summary		
Step 1	– Visual and descriptive report on findings	

Source: Own elaboration (accessed 09.07.2024).

"Economics, Econometrics and Finance" but no specific timeframe of publication was set. The review was limited to peer-reviewed articles only as they are commonly recognized as reliable and accepted scientific resources (Evers et al., 2023; Podsakoff et al., 2005). Any duplicates were excluded. The timespan of publication was not set as the intent of Phase 1 was to identify how the keywords overlaid in time and what linkages would be observable, so a wide dataset was acceptable.

There is a significant discrepancy in reference to the number of publications relating to GVCs and the specific megatrends. The most frequent one was the sustainability trajectory which dominantly included environmental issues. The digitalization megatrend has been gaining interest from 2020 which coincides with the COVID-19 pandemic. The geopolitical megatrend is still under-researched with only few publications appearing each year (Figure 3.3).

The interest in the GVCs and megatrends lays mostly within Western European institutions, U.S., China, and India (Figure 3.4). The geopolitical perspective dominated in the United Kingdom (Brexit). In terms of sustainability and digitalization most papers were published in *Journal of Cleaner Production*, *Supply Chain Management*, *Ecological Economics*, and *International Journal of Operations and Production Management*. The geopolitics-related query generated too few results to conduct similar analysis.

Figures 3.3 and 3.4 have shown that there is rising interest in the phenomenon. Therefore, with use of VOSviewer software bibliographic coupling analysis was carried out. The co-occurrence network map was established by analysing the abstracts and keywords of the papers. With the minimum number of keyword occurrences set to five, four clusters were delineated (Figure 3.5):

- Cluster 1: *Internationalization of GVCs* where the keyword is "international trade"; this cluster focuses on how the GVCs are organized geographically and how geopolitics influences the existing status quo,
- Cluster 2: *Climate change and GVCs* where the keyword is "sustainable development"; this cluster focuses on how specific subject areas (waste management, carbon emissions, etc.) impact GVC reconfiguration,
- Cluster 3: *Sustainable supply chains* where the keyword is "supply chain management"; this cluster focuses on how procurement is organised to embrace sustainability issues,
- Cluster 4: *Digitally sustainable GVCs* where the key word is "sustainability"; this cluster is the widest and most diversified. It focuses on different ways, including digital transformation, to reconfigure GVCs in a sustainable way.

What is important is that all of the identified clusters have overlapping focus areas. This proves that the contemporary megatrends are not separate or devoid of mutual impact. The geopolitical changes related to sustainability issues, sustainability related to digitalization, etc.

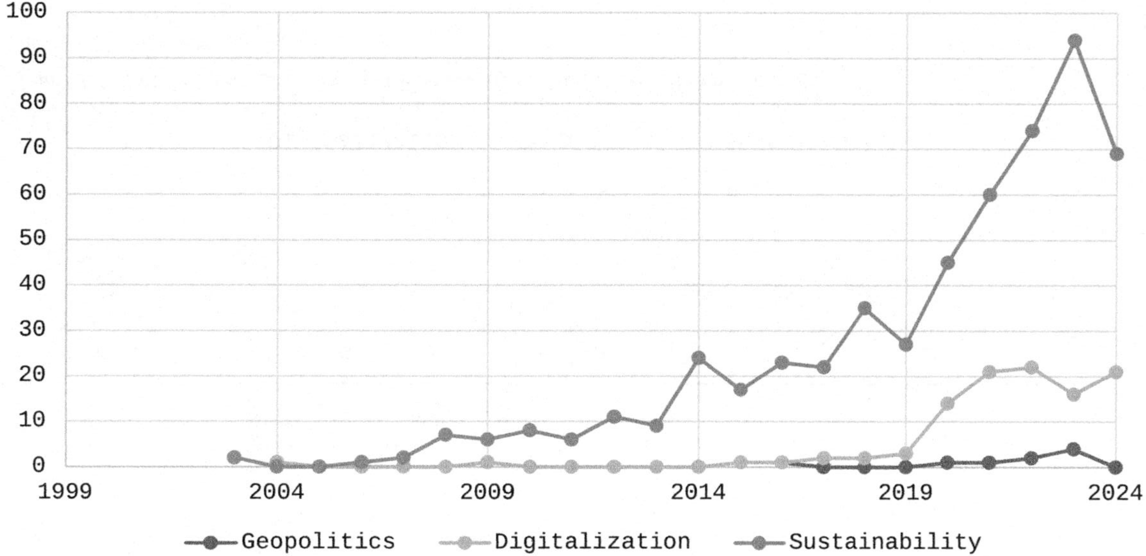

Figure 3.3 Number of publications in GVC and megatrends.

Source: Own elaboration.

Note: 2024 – data till July 2024.

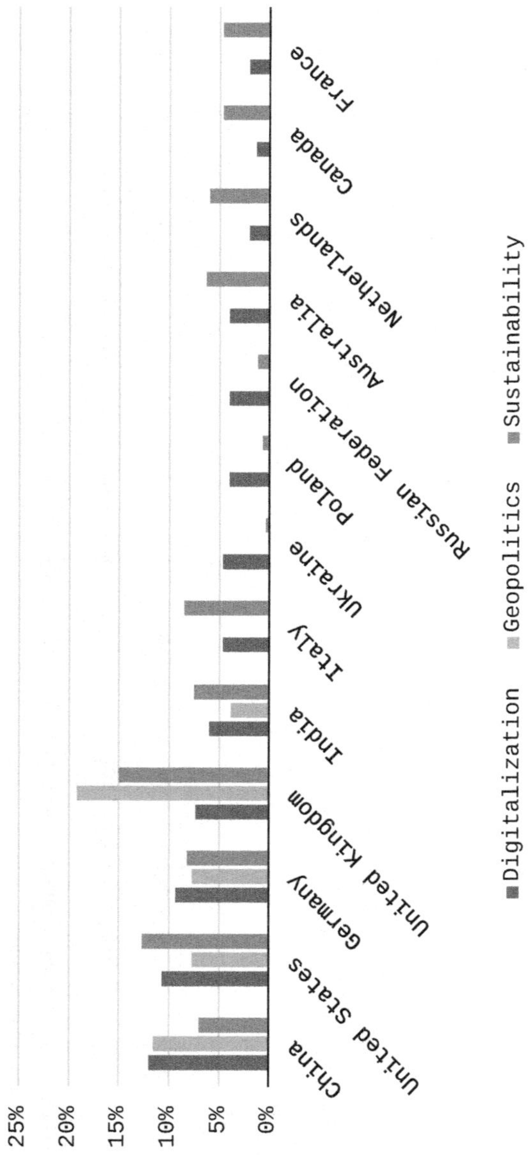

Figure 3.4 GVCs and megatrends – publications by country (% of all publications).

Source: Own elaboration.

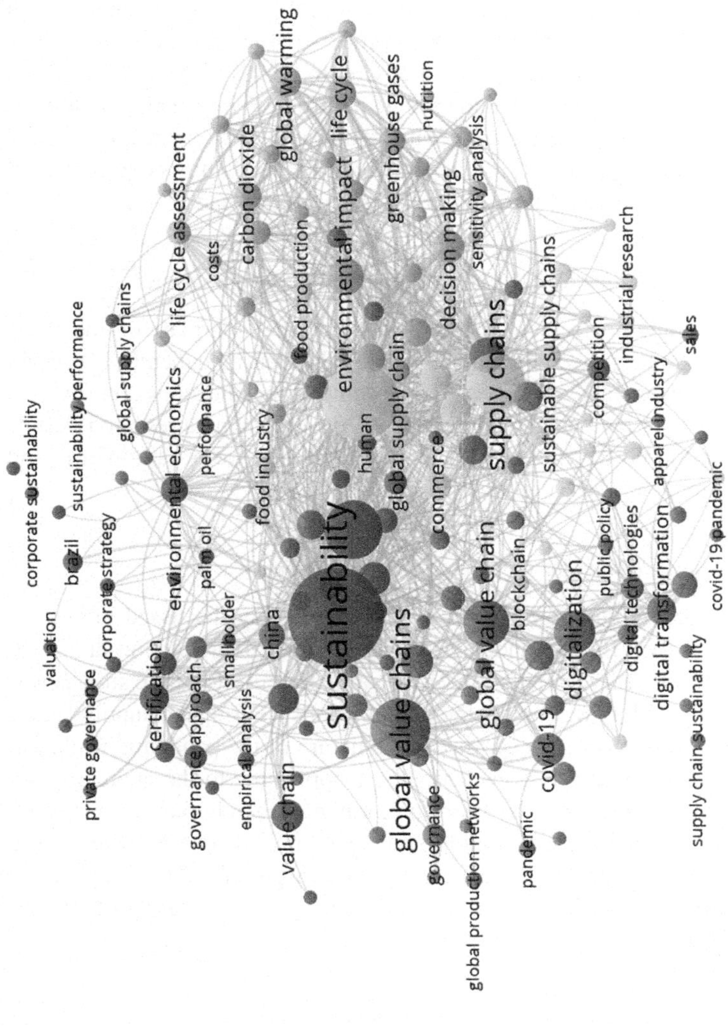

Figure 3.5 Co-occurrence key network.

The second phase of study was intended to carry out an in-depth analysis of those papers where the three trends were overlying. The final sample was derived from the initial search and included twelve papers. The papers were downloaded and subsequently uploaded to Zotero software to facilitate the analytical progress. Throughout the analysis the inductive theorizing process (Miles & Huberman, 1994) and flexible approach (Strauss & Corbin, 1998) were introduced. As a result a synthesis summarizing the articles' information, methodology, and key finding was created that was used to create an overview of main areas studied in the papers (Table 3.2). This was intended to identify potential future research directions and gaps.

Future studies on GVC and megatrends' intersection?

The literature review has showed that the interplay of the three megatrends is becoming more visible. The identified themes overlap in some elements, yet they still leave some of the questions unanswered. To further the understanding of GVC development, a research agenda is proposed that merges the themes identified from bibliometric and content analyses (Figure 3.6).

Research agenda for GVC reconfiguration trajectory

The reconfiguration of GVCs has been widely discussed in context of the COVID-19 pandemics (Dachs et al., 2019; Kano et al., 2022; Matysek-Jędrych et al., 2022). The aim of majority of the studies was to establish how to make the organizations, GVCs, and supply chains more resilient. However due to the nature of the pandemic itself, not all solutions and lessons learned are applicable to the contemporary disruptive megatrends. Therefore, a new research avenue emerges – what are the reconfiguration strategies applied by GVCs and companies in response to the contemporary megatrends? Is digitalization supportive in GVC reconfiguration or is the impact negligible in face of geopolitical disruptions?

Research agenda for GVC reconfiguration process

The rewiring of GVCs entails a substantial level of complexity and can prove crucial for future development however thus far has been given least attention. Choosing if and how to reconfigure the GVC

Table 3.2 Overlapping themes and issues addressed (n=12)

Theme	*Highlights*	*Methods applied*	*References*
Risk mitigation and GVCs	– Geopolitical tensions as key factor in increasing strategic and operational risk – Need for collaborative platform/framework to enhance and control trade, – Efficiency and resilience as inherent features of contemporary GVCs, – Increase of opportunistic behaviour	Empirical and conceptual	(Ghorbani et al., 2024; Hoekman et al., 2023; Inomata & Hanaka, 2024; Krykavskyy et al., 2023; Ploom et al., 2022)
Geographical reconfiguration of GVCs	– Increase of significance of geopolitical decoupling – Relocation strategies application: backshoring, nearshoring, and friendshoring – Changes in spatial division of labour – Changes in foreign direct investment (FDI) decision-making process – Pressure to achieve SDGs and comply with environmental regulations	Empirical and conceptual	(Blažek & Lypianin, 2024; Luo & Van Assche, 2023; Van Meeteren & Kleibert, 2022; Yang & Dong, 2016; Zhao et al., 2023)
Policy enforcement and their impact of GVCs	– Geopolitical prioritization – Observable paradigm shift to intervention-oriented techno-nationalism – Decline of multilateralism and role of institutions	Conceptual, overview of policies	(Guan & Xu, 2021; Luo & Van Assche, 2023; Seyfi & Hall, 2020; Yang & Dong, 2016)
Resource management in GVCs	– Potential rise of regional/allay trade blocs – Pressure to decarbonize and meet SDGs – Rise of geopolitical agenda to trade key resources	Empirical and conceptual	(Ghorbani et al., 2024; Luo & Van Assche, 2023; Zhao et al., 2023)

Source: Own elaboration.

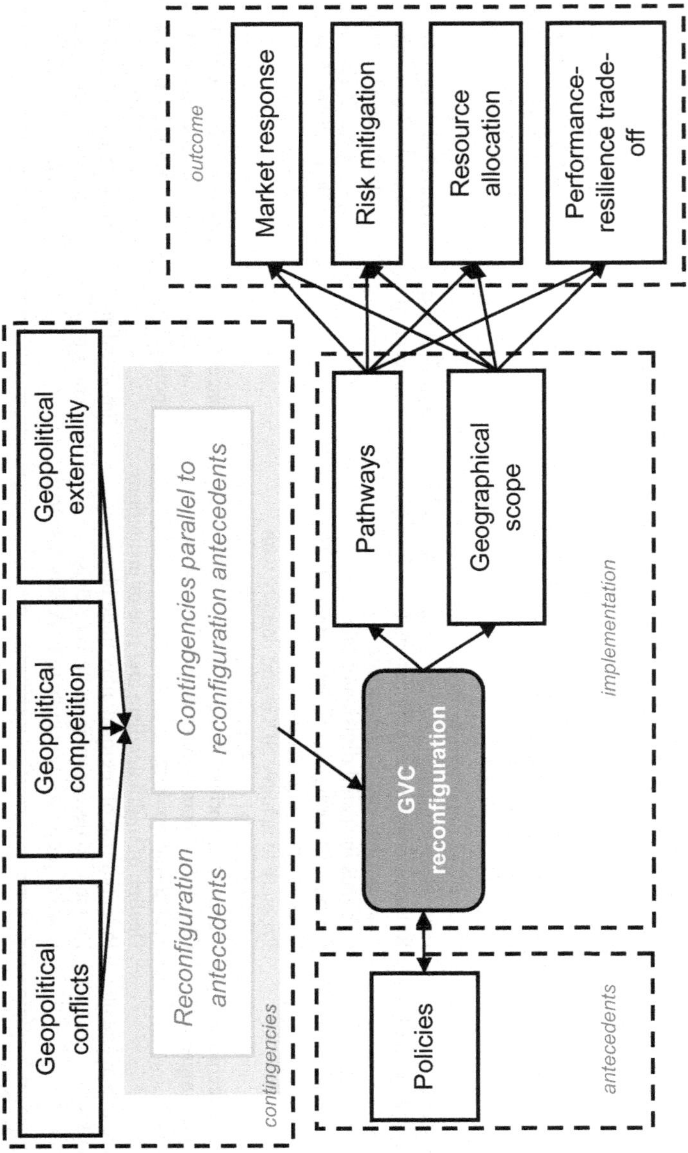

Figure 3.6 Concept mapping framework.
Source: Own elaboration.

network is one question, however how the process unfolds, including its duration, pace, and execution remain underexplored. The studies should explore what factors hinder or facilitate the implementation of GVC reconfiguration. Research should engage in the GVC disintegration stages, choice of relocation host country, and reconfiguration effectiveness and efficiency.

Research agenda for policy enforcement

The literature review suggests that policy enforcement has been recognized in research however most papers related to specific regulations, e.g. the Chip Act (Luo & Van Assche, 2023). Given the contemporary geopolitical tensions, the focus is set on multi- and bi-lateral trade arrangements and incentives to relocate the manufacturing process as well as inability of global institutions to perform their role (e.g. WTO). However, what is evident is that so far each megatrend has been treated separately, neglecting the fact that companies have to simultaneously consider both climate change-targeted policy acts and geopolitical limitations. Hence, new research question emerges on whether Sustainable Development Goals (SDG)-driven policy acts are aligned with trade policies or are they mutually exclusive? Can resilient GVCs be achieved through following SDG-related policies or geopolitical changes in trade arrangements or both at the same time?

Note

1 For search purpose "digital transformation" was substituted with "digitalization" and "climate change" with "sustainability". The decision to use wider terms was purposeful as due to indexing reasons these keywords generated more relevant and broader results.

4 Geopolitical distress and GVCs' resilience

Towards reconfiguration?

Richard Baldwin, in his speech on global value chains (GVCs) presented a bold, yet compelling argument that the current economic landscape in truth cannot be captured by the term "global value chains". He noted that economy is hardly global but rather divided into regional blocs, the notion of manufacturing process as a sequence of linear activities outdated and what matters is not the "value" that is created but the jobs that are being generated (Inomata, 2017). To top this up, the most recent crises have exposed the fragility of the GVCs, leaving the dominant economic model of the last three decades under rigorous investigation.

This chapter examines how GVCs are being reconfigured to address contemporary challenges. The current geopolitical context is first defined, and a new typology is proposed that includes geopolitical conflict, competition, and externality. Similarities and differences among these categories are outlined, supported by illustrative examples. The drivers behind GVC redesign are then analysed from both global and European perspectives, identifying factors that have compelled firms to reconsider production networks. Alternative pathways for restructuring GVCs are discussed, highlighting strategic options available under uncertainty. Attention then shifts to Central and Eastern Europe, where findings from a 2023 study of manufacturing firms are presented. Using the MCDM-ISM methodology, the pathways chosen by these firms to mitigate vulnerabilities and enhance resilience are mapped. These insights are subsequently cross-referenced with existing research on corporate strategies, offering a comparative view of global and regional adaptation. This integrated approach provides a comprehensive understanding of GVC reconfiguration as

DOI: 10.4324/9781003724803-4

both a response to geopolitical threats and a proactive strategy for long-term resilience.

Geopolitics and GVC reconfiguration

Looking back, the United Kingdom's (UK) decision to exit the European Union (EU) on 23 June 2016, otherwise known as Brexit, initiated years of uncertainty for businesses, marked by labour and inventory shortages. Shortly after, Donald Trump's presidential victory in the U.S., under the "Make America Great Again" campaign, prompted the manufacturing companies to relocate from China, supposedly back to the home country. The trade conflict with China that followed led to "tariff battle" that affected key trade commodities. The situation was further complicated by the COVID-19 pandemic in late 2019, which triggered another shift towards protectionism that was however restricted to certain product types, mostly vaccines, Personal Protective Equipment (PPE) and foodstuff. The Russian invasion of Ukraine in 2022 led to soaring oil and gas prices and disrupted a key trade route, triggering an energy crisis across Europe (Bednarski et al., 2023). A looming China–Taiwan conflict that may yet escalate, leads Western countries to act on how and where from to source chips and semiconductors. Shipment through the Red Sea route has collapsed due to Houthi rebels' attacks leading vessels to seek alternative routes and delaying delivery schedules. The existing and potential conflicts have caused the 2024 and 2025 Global Risk Report (Cavaciuti-Wishart et al., 2024) to predict that geopolitics-related risks will remain as the top threats for the upcoming short- and long-term perspective. In the upcoming years, it is anticipated that the world's resources and focus will concentrate primarily on three critical regions: Ukraine, Israel, and Taiwan. Should any of these areas experience an escalation of conflict, it could lead to significant upheaval in GVCs, financial systems, security arrangements, and political equilibrium, profoundly impacting the security as well as economic development of countries. Since the focus of dominant powers needs to be stretched among multiple fronts, conflict contagion is a key concern.

The abovementioned events differ in nature, scope and impact, yet all depict examples of geopolitical contingencies (Table 4.1). They all refer to events loaded with high level of uncertainty, volatility, and potential for causing societal, economic, or even military disruptions (Bednarski et al., 2023). Geopolitical contingencies cause shifts in

Table 4.1 Geopolitical contingencies – typology

Type	*Geopolitical conflict*	*Geopolitical competition*	*Geopolitical externality*
Definition	Inter-state conflict or military dispute that stems from political, economic, or cultural differences often leading to open territorial disputes	Inter-state rivalry that stems from power struggle to achieve strategic advantage	Independent occurrence of global or regional character that leads to inter-state policy responses
Key features	– Military actions – Resource competition – Historical, cultural, and religious triggers	– Hybrid actions and disinformation – Resource competition – Power struggle in geopolitical multiverse	– External occurrences unrelated to geopolitics – Black swans
GVC impact	– Competition for commodities – Logistics – Operational capacity and safety	– Competition for commodities – Cost efficiency – Trade blocks, trade barriers, and sanctions	– Protectionism – Nationalism – Trade barriers and restrictive policies
Example	Russian invasion in Ukraine	U.S.–China tensions and trade war	COVID-19 and trade restrictions

Source: Own elaboration.

international relationships and policies (including trade agreements and diplomacy) as well as global and regional power dynamics. In the context of GVCs, geopolitical contingencies impact risk and cause business adjustments, such as relocating production or diversifying suppliers in response to trade tensions or sanctions. Geopolitical conflict is characterized mostly through use of military forces, whereas geopolitical competition is more focused on the ascertaining power through non-military resources. The geopolitical externality on the other hand is mostly related to an event or occurrence that originally does not have a geological dimension but through its roll-out can cause a geopolitical dispute.

Changes in the global trade environment have historically occurred gradually. From 1995 onwards, no single country has seen its share of the annual worldwide export fluctuate by more than two percent. Even with recent market upheavals, the rate of change has remained consistent with this slow-moving trend (Seong et al., 2024). Yet, once we look at the geometry of these changes – considering the intensity, geographical and geopolitical distances as well as concentration – some significant shifts appear. Beginning in 2017, the trade dynamics of China, Germany, the UK, and the U.S. have seen a decrease in geopolitical distance.[1] The U.S. specifically has broadened its trade directions whilst also focusing on trade partners that are geographically closer. Despite these changes, the overall trade intensity among these developed countries remained relatively stable. Association of Southeast Asian Nations (ASEAN) countries, along with Brazil and India, have intensified trade activities, engaging in relationships with countries more geopolitically diverse and geographically distanced, thus redesigning their roles in global value chains (Figure 4.1). However, only the U.S. so far has significantly engaged in the reshoring practices, specifically in nearshoring, redirecting its trade and investment to closer countries.

In 2022, the worldwide inflow of foreign direct investment (FDI) saw a reduction of 12% to a total of $1.3 trillion. A series of global crises and challenges, including the conflict in Ukraine, escalating food and energy costs, looming recession threats, and mounting debt burdens across various nations, had an adverse impact on FDI globally. The international project financing and cross-border mergers and acquisitions (M&As) felt the impact acutely, with tighter financing conditions, increasing interest rates, and market uncertainties (*World Investment Report 2023*, 2024). Although the investment volumes dropped, the structure and destinations of FDI were not drastically altered, suggesting a cautious FDI approach without significant strategic changes (Jankowska et al., 2024). The recent data shows however that the regionalization of value chains might become more evident as the geopolitical threats unfold; the FDI destined for Europe originates mostly from Europe itself, and advanced European economies invest in Latin America and the U.S. and Canada as well. Although, Asia and Pacific as well as Africa experience more diversified sources of FDI inflow (Figure 4.2), the vast share of capital comes from the so-called Eastern countries (Seong et al., 2024) fuelling the debate on decoupling phenomenon.

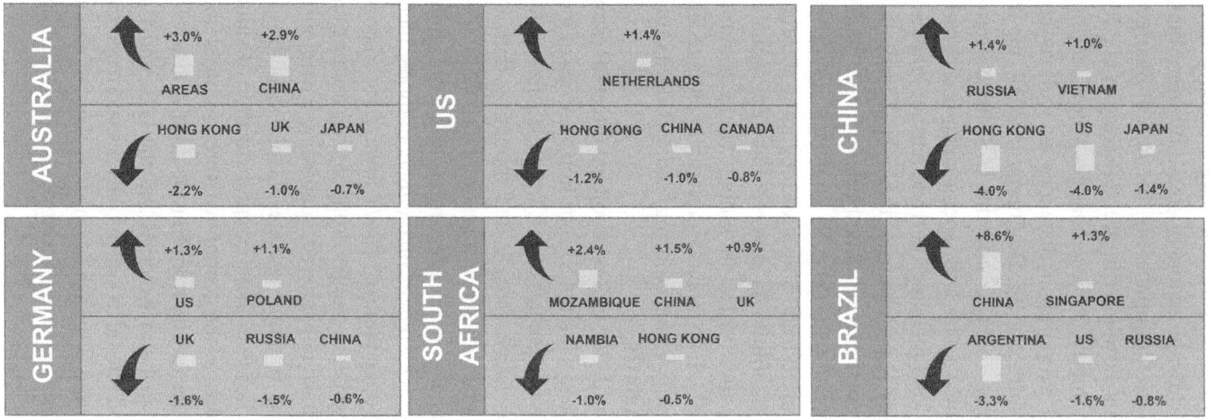

Figure 4.1 Percentage point change in exports share between 2017 and 2023, selected economies.

Source: Own elaboration based on Comtrade Database (2024).

Africa	Advanced Asia	Central Asia and Middle East	Advanced Europe	Developing Europe	Latin America	US & Canada	Rest of Asia and Pacific
Diverse sources	Diverse sources	Diverse sources	Advanced Europe	Advanced Europe	Advanced Europe	Advanced Europe & Asia	Diverse sources

Figure 4.2 Sources of highest investment flows 2022–2023.

Source: Own elaboration based on Seong et al. (2024).

European reconfiguration landscape – recent developments

The relocation (including reshoring, nearshoring, and friendshoring) was expected to become the answer to the rewiring of the GVCs. However, the measurement of the relocation scope remains problematic (Krenz & Strulik, 2021). Various approach to operationalizing the concepts include the changes in employment and creation of new job (both directly in manufacturing and indirectly through back-office), changes in investment as well as other qualitative measures, like press announcements and industry reports. Therefore, providing an unambiguous answer to whether relocation is as common as was anticipated, remains troublesome.

Yet, certain international institutions, including for instance Reshoring Institute or The Vienna Institute for International Economic Studies, follow the global trends and provide and approximation of the relocation scope. According to their analyses, relocation has been most visible in case of the U.S. since reshoring and nearshoring are used as part of their geoeconomic strategy and political agenda. Reshoring Initiative (2023) reported that in 2021 reshoring exceeded the FDI (based on the measure of job announcements) in the U.S. for the second year in the row and that the trend was expected to be upkept. For more than decade China has accounted for almost 70% of the reshoring to the U.S., followed by relocations from Mexico and Canada (Figure 4.3).

The scope of the relocation in Europe is however smaller (Delis et al., 2019). The scale of the phenomenon is less closely tracked than in the case of the U.S. and the reports tend to focus on the specific subregions. For instance Deloitte (2023) reports that most companies in Central Europe increased collaboration with their suppliers, at the same time diversifying their range. However, every fifth of the studied manufacturing companies has claimed to have relocated its production plants back to the region. Hadwick (2023) studied the intensions of European companies that declared their willingness to relocate sourcing and operations. According to his studies Central and Eastern European (CEE) countries, specifically Poland and Germany where the most commonly declared locations for nearshoring or reshoring activities (Figure 4.4).

Reshoring and nearshoring in Europe still remain a subtle trend rather than the expected megashift. Although the mostly referred to driver for the relocation are now geopolitical tensions, the decision is

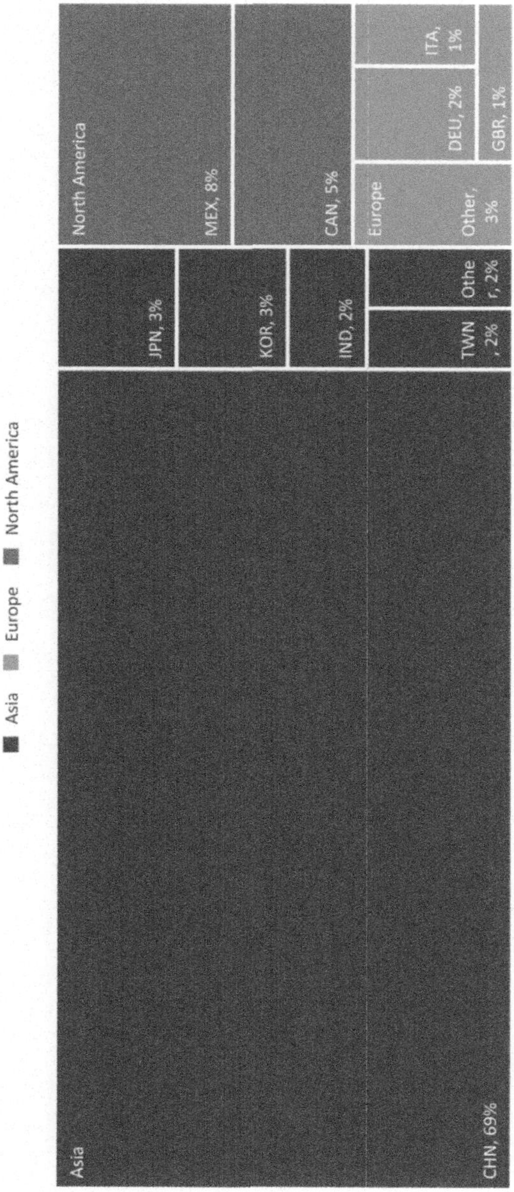

Figure 4.3 Reshoring to the U.S. market (2010–2022), by original investment country.

Source: Own elaboration based on Reshoring Initiative 2022 Data Report (2023).

Figure 4.4 Mapping the relocation of European companies (2022).

Source: Own elaboration based on Hadwick (2023).

still based on cost reduction and increased economic efficiency. The recent Savills 2024 Nearshoring Index ranked 26 countries according to their economic resilience, costs, business ecosystem and ESG compliance. The European locations, especially Portugal, Czechia, Poland, and Sweden, have been identified as the most nearshoring-friendly locations (Rushton, 2024). Portugal and Czech Republic ranked similar in 2022 Index but Poland and Sweden have significantly improved their positions.[2] Theoretically, the nearshoring to CEE should gain momentum however there are important pitfalls that hinder the relocation process (Halesiak, 2024):

- regulatory ecosystem – although industrialization, including relocation, is claimed to be supported in the EU, the actual programmes and plans favour alternative solutions like aggregated procurement and strategic alliances,
- labour and skills shortage – up-skilling and re-skilling is needed to rebuild competencies in relocating industries,
- infrastructural and resource issues – water, electricity, and land availability are under threat, especially considering the green transition, which necessitates new investments to meet environmental protection standards,
- increased risk and dependencies – Europe's dependence on rare earth metals and other strategic materials cannot be easily substituted making the production reliable especially on China; alternative trade agreements are prone to geopolitical risks that is intensified by unstable demand making the forecasting difficult,
- high entry barriers – certain industries (e.g. competition) require distinctive capabilities that are not easily replicated in the regional environment,
- power struggle – Europe as a region has to actively compete against alternative locations, such as the U.S. that offer substantial governmental subsidies through regulatory frameworks (e.g. the U.S. Inflation Reduction Act (IRA), CHIPS and Science Act).

GVCs incorporate elements of both competition and cooperation, as well as a mix of absolute and relative advantages. The interplay of benefits and expenses can be generated both through supply and demand channels. Consequently, GVCs may not only fall victim to geopolitical uncertainties but can also contribute to their escalation by (Solingen et al., 2021):

- intensifying the existing uncertainty – a flagship example of the phenomenon was demonstrated by the trade war between the U.S. and China that led to an increase in the "trade policy uncertainty index" (Ahir et al., 2019); the retaliatory tariffs and tensions are estimated to have added ca. 20% to the uncertainty since 2016,
- rising geopolitical tensions and mistrust between major powers, notably the U.S. and China – threat to GVCs reliant on data-driven technologies like AI, IoT, and cloud computing. These technologies require globalized markets and mutual trust, but growing nationalism and unilateralism have weakened confidence in international institutions that traditionally facilitated cooperation and reduced uncertainty. While regional agreements such as Comprehensive and Progressive Agreement for Trans-Pacific Partnership (CPTPP) and Regional Comprehensive Economic Partnership (RCEP) offer some hope for restoring trust, overall, the viability of complex, data-centric GVCs is increasingly at risk,
- inward-looking policies and rising political costs – populist narratives and mistrust frame GVCs as serving foreign interests, making self-reliance politically attractive and costly to reverse. While decoupling undermines competitiveness and employment, it also risks trapping industrializing economies in middle-income stagnation, reducing the promised gains from global integration,
- "vertical contagion" through retaliatory measures such as tariffs, sanctions, export controls, and technology restrictions, creating spiralling disputes among major economies. Policies like China's push for tech self-sufficiency and U.S. reshoring strategies have triggered tit-for-tat responses, undermining global cooperation and limiting access to critical inputs and markets. These dynamics often lead to vicious cycles of decoupling, escalating costs, and suboptimal outcomes for all parties involved,
- "horizontal contagion" by spreading disruptions across upstream and downstream nodes of GVCs and even to third-party participants. Measures such as tariff barriers, subsidies, and retaliatory trade practices trigger ripple effects throughout interconnected networks, amplifying instability and uncertainty across entire GVC ecosystems,
- reducing the mobility of people and expertise across GVC nodes, undermining critical human interactions that sustain services and intangible assets.

Reconfiguration and pathways' dependencies

As mentioned before, Strange and Humphrey (2019) claimed that if reconfiguration is considered, companies reach for either relocation strategies, supplier diversification and internal adjustments aimed at competitiveness creation or a mix of those decisions. Therefore, an attempt was made to see how companies incorporated these trajectories to the rewiring of their global activities and whether these decisions were anyhow interdependent. In April–June 2023, 50 manufacturing companies located in Poland but with global operations were investigated to see if and how they changed their activities, both in terms of their own manufacturing process and their embeddedness in the GVCs (Table 4.2).

The study was not conducted in reference to any specific geopolitical threat, yet companies reported to have taken action in face of the Russian invasion in Ukraine, the deterioration of the Taiwan situation and general polarization between "the West and the East". Following Strange and Humphrey (2019) and Sekliuckiene and Rybakovas (2023), three groups of reconfiguration strategies were identified (Table 4.3).

Table 4.2 Overview of experts' portfolio

Characteristics		*N*	*%*
Current industry represented	Division 10 – Manufacture of food products	6	12%
	Division 14 – Manufacture of wearing apparel	3	6%
	Division 17 – Manufacture of paper and paper products	6	12%
	Division 20 – Manufacture of chemicals and chemical products	8	16%
	Division 23 – Manufacture of other non-metallic mineral products	12	24%
	Division 27 – Manufacture of electrical equipment	15	30%
Experience in the industry	15–20	30	60%
	20–25	16	32%
	25+	4	8%
Position in the company	CEO	20	40%
	Head of procurement	18	36%
	Head of manufacturing	12	24%

Note: The positions in company vary by name therefore they were grouped according to the similarity of responsibilities carried out.

Table 4.3 GVC reconfiguration trajectories in face of geopolitical tensions

Group	*Name of strategic decision*	*Explanation*
Capacity building trajectory	F1 – Capacity and inventory buffers	Shifting from "just in time" to "just in case" approach by foregoing lean inventories in favour of surplus
	F2 – Optimizing production	Simplifying the manufacturing process by cutting out non-essential elements
	F10 – Implementing machine learning, AI and big data	Understanding and leveraging data to enhance efficiency and effectiveness
	F11 – Technology up-grading	Process automation through enhanced digitalization
	F12 – Alternative components	Temporarily producing certain products/components on demand, without long-term disruption to normal business processes
Relocation trajectory	F3 – Production nearshoring	Relocating manufacturing activities to near-home location
	F4 – Production reshoring	Relocating manufacturing activities to home location
	F5 – Manufacturing network diversification	Diversifying manufacturing bases (e.g. dual production mode)
Supplier diversification trajectory	F6 – Multisourcing (number)	Expanding the portfolio of suppliers number-wise
	F7 – Multisourcing (location)	Expanding the portfolio of suppliers location-wise
	F8 – Multisourcing (regional concentration)	Creating regional clusters of tier-1 and tier-2 suppliers
	F9 – Ecosystem partnerships	In-depth network collaboration with chosen strategic suppliers and service providers

Source: Own elaboration.

All of the strategic choices listed in Table 4.3 were reported as undertaken however with varied intensity. Most companies followed the supplier diversification trajectory (74%) whilst capacity building trajectory (48%) and the relocation pathway were significantly less common (42%). The aim of the study was to see whether the choices companies made were interdependent, i.e. whether implementing solutions in one strategic trajectory could drive companies to apply other trajectories as well. To this end the interpretive structural modelling (ISM) analysis was applied (Sorooshian et al., 2023). As part of the study respondents were asked to determine the pairwise relationships between the strategies. The aggregated structural self-interactive matrix (SSIM) was constructed based on the means of interviewees' individual input (Table 4.4). The pairwise relationship was considered according to a pattern:

- factor X is influenced by Y; however, Y is not influenced by X (A in SSIM matrix),
- factor Y is influenced by X; however, X is not influenced by Y (B in SSIM matrix),
- factors X and Y influence each other (Z in SSIM matrix),
- there is no contextual relationship between factors X and Y (O in SSIM matrix).

Next, a binary initial reachability matrix (IRM) was created based on the SSIM data by converting the symbols A, B, Z, and O to values 1 and 0 according to the pattern (Table 4.5):

- when the *(i,j)* relationship in the SSIM is A, the *(i,j)* entry in the IRM is set as "1" and the *(j,i)* as "0";

Table 4.4 Aggregated structural self-interactive matrix (SSIM)

	F1	*F2*	*F3*	*F4*	*F5*	*F6*	*F7*	*F8*	*F9*	*F10*	*F11*	*F12*
F1	-	O	O	O	O	O	O	B	O	O	O	O
F2		-	O	O	O	B	B	B	B	O	O	O
F3			-	O	O	O	A	O	O	O	O	O
F4				-	O	A	A	O	O	O	O	O
F5					-	Z	Z	Z	B	B	B	O
F6						-	A	O	B	B	B	O
F7							-	B	Z	B	B	O
F8								-	B	B	O	O
F9									-	O	O	O
F10										-	B	O
F11											-	O
F12												-

Source: Own elaboration.

Table 4.5 Initial reachability matrix (IRM)

	F1	*F2*	*F3*	*F4*	*F5*	*F6*	*F7*	*F8*	*F9*	*F10*	*F11*	*F12*
F1	1	0	0	0	0	0	0	0	0	0	0	0
F2	0	1	0	0	0	0	0	0	0	0	0	0
F3	0	0	1	0	0	0	1	0	0	0	0	0
F4	0	0	0	1	0	1	1	0	0	0	0	0
F5	0	0	0	0	1	1	1	1	0	0	0	0
F6	0	1	0	0	1	1	1	0	0	0	0	0
F7	0	1	0	0	1	0	1	0	1	0	0	0
F8	1	1	0	0	1	0	1	1	0	0	0	0
F9	0	1	0	0	1	1	1	1	1	0	0	0
F10	0	0	0	0	1	1	1	1	0	1	0	0
F11	0	0	0	0	1	1	1	0	0	1	1	0
F12	0	0	0	0	0	0	0	0	0	0	0	1

Source: Own elaboration.

- when the *(i,j)* relationship in the SSIM is B, the *(i,j)* entry in the IRM is set as "0" and the *(j,i)* as "1";
- when the *(i,j)* relationship in the SSIM is Z, both the *(i,j)* and *(j,i)* entries in the IRM are set as "1";
- when the *(i,j)* relationship in the SSIM is O, both the *(i,j)* and *(j,i)* entries in the IRM are set as "0";
- for diagonal relationships in the SSIM, the (i=j) entry in the IRM is set as "1".

Transitivity checks (Table 4.6) were applied to verify the consistency of the model, as suggested by Farris and Sage (1975), Sushil (2017) and Jena et al. (2016).

To conceptualize the IS model, the level partitioning of factors was carried out. The factors were ranked and divided to subsequent levels based on their reachability and antecedent sets (Table 4.7). The final reachability matrix and level partitioning allowed also for diagraph design (Figure 4.5).

Results of the study

The three trajectories seem only partially co-dependent. The relocation strategy is not driven by other strategic choices except for advanced technologies implementation such as artificial intelligence

Table 4.6 Final reachability matrix with transitivity checks

	F1	*F2*	*F3*	*F4*	*F5*	*F6*	*F7*	*F8*	*F9*	*F10*	*F11*	*F12*
F1	1	0	0	0	0	0	0	0	0	0	0	0
F2	0	1	0	0	0	0	0	0	0	0	0	0
F3	1*	1*	1	0	1*	1*	1	1*	1*	0	0	0
F4	1*	1*	0	1	1*	1	1	1*	1*	0	0	0
F5	1*	1*	0	0	1	1	1	1	1*	0	0	0
F6	1*	1	0	0	1	1	1	1*	1*	0	0	0
F7	1*	1	0	0	1	1*	1	1*	1	0	0	0
F8	1	1	0	0	1	1*	1	1	1*	0	0	0
F9	1*	1	0	0	1	1	1	1	1	0	0	0
F10	1*	1*	0	0	1	1	1	1	1*	1	0	0
F11	1*	1*	0	0	1	1	1	1*	1*	1	1	0
F12	0	0	0	0	0	0	0	0	0	0	0	1

* transitivity
Source: Own elaboration.

and machine learning. At the same time however relocation strategy strongly drives the supplier diversification trajectory. This is not surprising as any production-related choices are bound to entail changes in the procurement process. The relationships are mostly indirect which means that the decision makers are not fully aware of their existence even though they prevail. The supplier diversification factors are called the linkage strategies as they both drive the capacity building trajectory and are dependent on the relocation factors and technology up-grading as well as advanced technology implementation. The capacity building trajectory is the most heterogenous in nature. It includes pure drivers which influence other strategies but are not anyhow dependent on them (these are technology-related factors), dependable strategies which are highly influenced by the interplay of other strategies (relocation and supplier base) and even autonomous factor which remains outside the interdependency matrix. The latter one is the implementation of alternative components which companies tend to reach for as an independent process (Table 4.8).

In the midst of the pandemic UNCTAD (2020) expected that GVCs would develop along four possible trajectories: diversification, replication, reshoring, or regionalization. Diversification essentially meant upholding global production networks but with significantly more profound local contribution. The multinational enterprises (MNEs) were

Table 4.7 Level partitioning

F	*Reachability*	*Antecedents*	*Intersection*	*L*
Iteration 1				
F1	F1	F1, F3, F4, F5, F6, F7, F8, F9, F10, F11	F1	I
F2	F2	F2, F3, F4, F5, F6, F7, F8, F9, F10, F11	F2	I
F3	F1, F2, F3, F5, F6, F7, F8, F9	F3	F3	
F4	F1, F2, F4, F5, F6, F7, F8, F9	F4	F4	
F5	F1, F2, F5, F6, F7, F8, F9	F3, F4, F5, F6, F7, F8, F9, F10, F11	F5, F6, F7, F8, F9	
F6	F1, F2, F5, F6, F7, F8, F9	F3, F4, F5, F6, F7, F8, F9, F10, F11	F5, F6, F7, F8, F9	
F7	F1, F2, F5, F6, F7, F8, F9	F3, F4, F5, F6, F7, F8, F9, F10, F11	F5, F6, F7, F8, F9	
F8	F1, F2, F5, F6, F7, F8, F9	F3, F4, F5, F6, F7, F8, F9, F10, F11	F5, F6, F7, F8, F9	
F9	F1, F2, F5, F6, F7, F8, F9	F3, F4, F5, F6, F7, F8, F9, F10, F11	F5, F6, F7, F8, F9	
F10	F1, F2, F5, F6, F7, F8, F9, F10	F10, F11	F10	
F11	F1, F2, F5, F6, F7, F8, F9, F10, F11	F11	F11	
F12	F12	F12	F12	I
Iteration 2				
F3	F3, F5, F6, F7, F8, F9	F3	F3	
F4	F4, F5, F6, F7, F8, F9	F4	F4	
F5	F5, F6, F7, F8, F9	F3, F4, F5, F6, F7, F8, F9, F10, F11	F5, F6, F7, F8, F9	II
F6	F5, F6, F7, F8, F9	F3, F4, F5, F6, F7, F8, F9, F10, F11	F5, F6, F7, F8, F9	II
F7	F5, F6, F7, F8, F9	F3, F4, F5, F6, F7, F8, F9, F10, F11	F5, F6, F7, F8, F9	II
F8	F5, F6, F7, F8, F9	F3, F4, F5, F6, F7, F8, F9, F10, F11	F5, F6, F7, F8, F9	II
F9	F5, F6, F7, F8, F9	F3, F4, F5, F6, F7, F8, F9, F10, F11	F5, F6, F7, F8, F9	II
F10	F5, F6, F7, F8, F9, F10	F10, F11	F10	
F11	F5, F6, F7, F8, F9, F10, F11	F11	F11	
Iteration 3				
F3	F3	F3	F3	III
F4	F4	F4	F4	III

Table 4.7 (Continued)

F	*Reachability*	*Antecedents*	*Intersection*	*L*
F10	F10	F10, F11	F10	III
F11	F10, F11	F11	F11	
Iteration 4				
F11	F11	F11	F11	IV

Source: Own elaboration.

expected to leverage the I4.0 solutions to that purpose. Replication trajectory – although discussed – was not likely to be realized due to high implementation costs. It entailed launching multiple "twin facilities" across many countries to perform similar activities. Reshoring trajectory meant relocating back to home country to ensure shorter and less fragmented GVCs. In effect domestic value chains (DVCs) were expected to raise. The scenario also included the option of either nearshoring or friendshoring, which should have given rise to regional value chains (RVCs) under the regionalization trajectory. Both strategies are based on relocation however the geographical scope differs. UNCTAD (2020) predicted that under geopolitical threat GVCs would only follow either reshoring or regionalization paths. Yet our results indicate that three out of four suggested alternatives were implemented: relocation (both reshoring and regionalization) and diversification (Table 4.9). This was supplemented by one other solution where MNEs opted to uphold the existing status quo whilst investing in operational capacity (capacity building trajectory).

Similar conclusion were drawn by Pedersen et al. (2024) who surveyed 189 Danish manufacturing companies with international operations. They identified various resilience strategies employed by MNEs as a response to recent disruptions and megatrends, including scanning strategy, robustness strategy, and redundancy strategy. The scanning strategy was similar to the capacity building trajectory where emphasis was laid on the application of advanced technology and analytical tools to ensure quick response to any disruptions. This strategy was especially useful in volatile markets prone to experience geopolitical instability and information distortion. The robustness strategy was again drawing on our capacity building trajectory but it was applied mostly in face of temporary disruptions, such as natural disasters. The key element of this strategy was allocating the financial

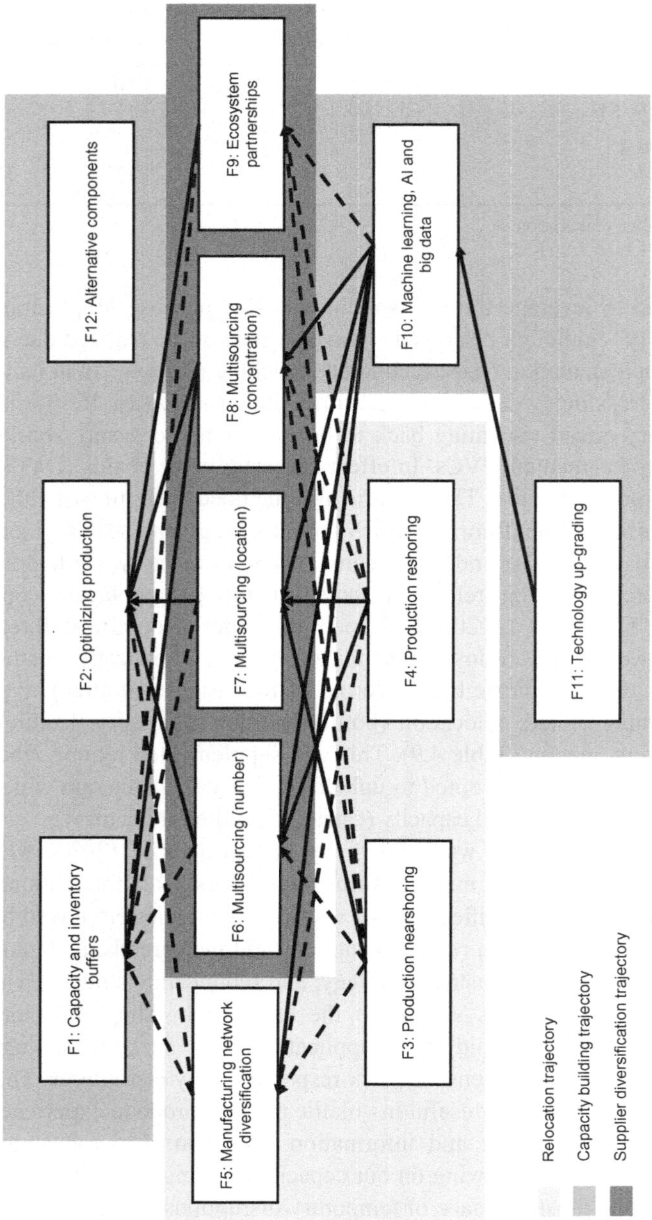

Figure 4.5 GVC reconfiguration trajectories – dependencies and interactions.
Source: Own elaboration.

Table 4.8 MICMAC analysis of the strategies

Group	*Name of strategic decision*	*Driving power*	*Dependency*	*Character*
Capacity building trajectory	F1 – Capacity and inventory buffers	1	10	Dependent
	F2 – Optimizing production	1	10	Dependent
	F10 – Implementing machine learning, AI, and big data	8	2	Driving
	F11 – Technology up-grading	9	1	Driving
	F12 – Alternative components	1	1	Autonomous
Relocation trajectory	F3 – Production nearshoring	8	1	Driving
	F4 – Production reshoring	8	1	Driving
	F5 – Manufacturing network diversification	7	9	Linkage
Supplier diversification trajectory	F6 – Multisourcing (number)	7	9	Linkage
	F7 – Multisourcing (location)	7	9	Linkage
	F8 – Multisourcing (regional concentration)	7	9	Linkage
	F9 – Ecosystem partnerships	7	9	Linkage

Source: Own elaboration.

Table 4.9 Pre-pandemic vs post-pandemic predictions on international production trajectories under geopolitical strain

	Diversification	*Replication*	*Reshoring*	*Regionalization*	*Capacity building*
Expected			+	+	
Observed	+		+	+	+

Source: Own elaboration based on (Elia et al., 2021).

and managerial resources to recover from the disruptions in a timely manner. However, no major GVC reconfiguration steps were normally undertaken. The final strategy, known as redundancy strategy included both the relocation trajectory and supplier diversification trajectory. Pedersen et al. (2024) indicate that both geographical replication and supplier replication are most probable when permanent disruptions involving trade conflicts and regional disputes are in question. Redundancy strategy is costly as it genuinely rewires the GVCs configuration.

Notes

1 Geopolitical distance measure was created by McKinsey Global Institute by providing the value-weighted average trade partner distance based on United Nations General Assembly voting patterns.

2 The 2022 ranking included 54 countries. However Poland and Sweden gained positions over countries that were ranked in both studies.

5 Relocation as a GVC reconfiguration trajectory

The transfer of value chain activities from a company's home country to foreign locations, known as offshoring, for decades attracted the attention of scholars who studied the links between multinational enterprises (MNEs) internationalization strategies, cost reduction, growth, and operational flexibility (Schmeisser, 2013). The phenomenon was well researched, pointing to disintegration advantages that were mostly attributed to the globalization effect. However, the late 2000s have brought the early signs of reshoring, defined by Fratocchi et al. (2014) as "the back relocation of earlier off-shored production activities". The process was triggered by the Global Financial Crisis (GFC) and intensified by other contingencies, including the geopolitical disruptions (Brexit, COVID-19 pandemic, U.S.–China trade war), technological advancements, policy shifts, and even sustainability efforts.

Although the phenomenon is well established in literature, reshoring is not reflected in official statistics which means that researchers use proxy measures to capture its extent. Most commonly, either secondary data or ad hoc surveys are applied. In Europe, the annual number of reshoring cases, identified either via media announcements or through changes in employment structures in home and host countries ranges between 2.6% and 21% (D'Ambrosio & Lavoratori, 2025).

Recent global developments including trade wars, armed conflicts, the pandemic, neonationalism, and transportation bottlenecks could further accelerate reshoring decisions. These decisions may not only serve as reactive measures to address performance issues or

DOI: 10.4324/9781003724803-5

GVC-related challenges in offshored locations, but also as proactive strategies to enhance GVC resilience and prevent future disruptions (Barbieri et al., 2020; Gereffi, 2020; Pedroletti & Ciabuschi, 2023). Companies are also seeing fewer incentives to offshore as the three main drivers behind the practice disappear: the advancements in ICT, reduction of trade costs and removal of political and economic barriers (D'Ambrosio & Lavoratori, 2025). As a result, relocation strategies may become an appealing alternative for firms safeguarding themselves from future vulnerabilities.

The results of the empirical study discussed in Chapter 4 have shown that relocation, including reshoring and nearshoring practices, are one of the key elements in the rewiring of GVCs. The empirical evidence tends to suggest that so far it was mostly the large companies that relocated their production facilities, yet the study of Antràs (2020) indicates that in the future reshoring may be dominantly used by the small and medium-sized enterprises (SMEs). In theory, reshoring becomes effective if the associated fixed costs are low (Martin et al., 2023), which is often the case of smaller firms when only part of the company's production has been offshored. Hence, the companies less deeply integrated into GVCs face lower fixed costs when relocating back home.

This chapter focuses on three elements; first, it conceptualizes reshoring, highlighting how it relates to other forms of relocation within GVC. Moreover, it explores different research perspectives of reshoring, indicating how and where they overlap. Second, it presents an empirical model based on Multiple Criteria Decision-Making (MCDM) method, which helps to identify the drives of reshoring under geopolitical uncertainty. Notably, the model reveals interrelations between factors, illustrating how a network of factors can collectively drive the relocation of a company. Finally, the results of the study are cross-referenced with the most discussed groups of reshoring antecedents found in literature.

Conceptualization of reshoring

To discuss the relocation concept under geopolitical strain, it is first worth to look into its conceptualization. Relocation is part of a wider research agenda that focuses on location choices (Hilmola et al., 2025). The literature identifies several terms that, while overlapping, carry distinct meanings. One such term is reshoring, also referred to as backshoring, which involves bringing production back to the home country. In some instances, researchers may also use this term to describe relocating production closer to the home country, a process more accurately termed nearshoring. Additionally, the concept of friendshoring refers to relocating operations to countries that are geopolitically aligned with the investor, though this may or may not overlap with nearshoring depending on the specific circumstances. Finally, rightshoring refers to relocating based on objective criteria designed to achieve an optimal location, without being influenced by geopolitical considerations (Table 5.1).

The research agenda on reshoring has long been concentrated on two interrelated but distinct perspectives: one sees it as a firm-level phenomenon, where companies adapt their manufacturing strategies in response to exogenous and endogenous changes, and the other views it as a regional-level phenomenon, where reshoring is seen as a way to enhance resilience and competitiveness within production networks (Figure 5.1). At the same time the phenomenon can be further broken down to three phases: the motives to reshore which include

Table 5.1 Conceptualizing relocation strategies

Term	*Definition*	*Examples*
Reshoring/ Backshoring	Bringing production or business operations back to the company's home country from overseas	Bosch moving appliance production from China back to Germany
Nearshoring	Relocating production to a nearby country, often sharing geographical, cultural, or economic ties with the home country	Boeing partnering with French manufacturer Safran to establish a wiring factory in Mexico, responsible for wiring in the 787 Dreamliner
Friendshoring	Moving supply chains to allied or politically friendly countries to reduce reliance on geopolitical rivals	U.S. companies shifting semiconductor production to India and Vietnam instead of China
Rightshoring	Placing production in the most optimal location based on cost, efficiency, and risk factors	Nike using a mix of factories in Vietnam, Indonesia, and the U.S. to optimize costs and logistics

Source: Own elaboration.

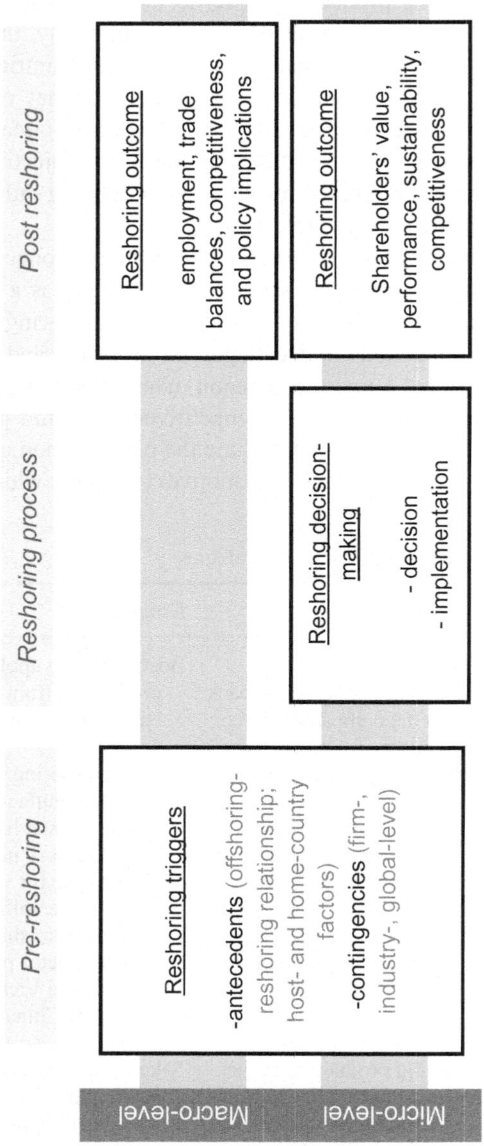

Figure 5.1 Reshoring research perspectives.

Source: Own elaboration based on Hilmola et al. (2025) and Pedroletti and Ciabuschi (2023).

both typical antecedents and more circumstantial contingencies, the reshoring decision process and the reshoring outcome. The first and last phases can be viewed from both macro and micro-perspectives whereas the process itself is generally focused on governance modes, implementation pace, scope of reshored activities and making it primarily a firm-level study.

Reshoring can entail relocating either full scope of company's activities (full reshoring) or only a part of them (partial reshoring) whether they are carried out by a company's own subsidiary or outsourced to foreign suppliers (Pedroletti, 2025). If we consider the relocation matrix by Gray et al. (2013), the reshoring outcome is dependent on both the location and ownership (governance mode) of the investment. Should the mix be expanded to include the scope of activities relocated, the complexities surrounding reshoring continue to grow as they embrace elements previously either not considered or not present when studying the phenomenon (Figure 5.2). Contemporary contingencies have highlighted the growing prominence of two strategies: dual structure and sourcing diversification (Mroczek-Dąbrowska et al. 2024). Dual structure refers to a reshoring strategy where the relocation was most commonly triggered by the weak GVC structure and accelerated by a certain contingency (e.g. geopolitical disturbance). In effect, the company maintains operations both in the initially offshored location and back in the home country. The dual model can be either temporary or permanent depending on the industry specificity. The sourcing diversification refers to a similar solution, where company simultaneously retains the offshored and reshored locations, however while outsourcing the operations.

The growing complexity of the reshoring phenomenon underlines the need for a thorough review of the current understanding of the topic. In the last decade, geopolitical disruptions have been identified as the primary contingency driving relocation choices. Hence, it is crucial to examine the full scope of reshoring phenomenon: identifying which antecedents remain relevant, which are no longer of key importance, and what new factors have emerged; understanding how the reshoring process itself has evolved; and finally analysing the resulting outcomes. The remainder of this chapter will focus on exploring reshoring antecedents under geopolitical strain, while Chapter 6 will discuss decisions related to reshoring implementation, including the final outcomes (location and governance mode) depicted on a case study.

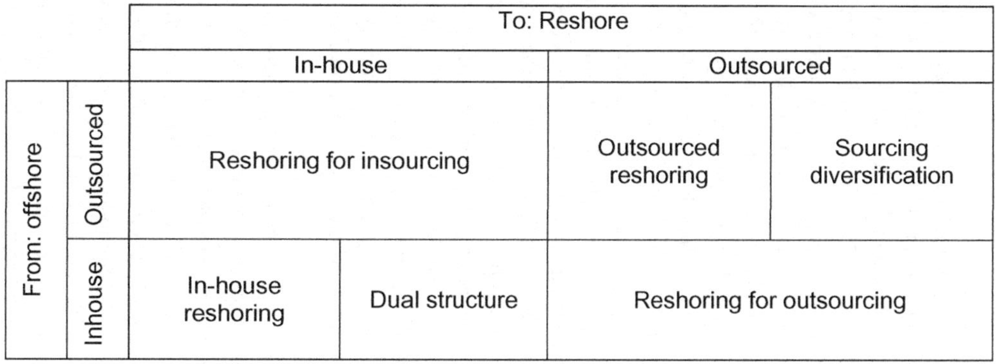

Figure 5.2 Reshoring mix – location, ownership, and scope.

Source: Own elaboration based on Gray et al. (2013).

Methods, data collection, and experts involved

MCDM methods are a set of techniques used for decision-making in situations where there are multiple, often conflicting, criteria to consider. Since the reshoring phenomenon fits this description, the analysis was conducted with use of one of the methods from the MCDM toolkit. The data was analysed with use of the Decision-Making Trial and Evaluation Laboratory (DEMATEL) technique, first developed by the Battelle Memorial Association in Geneva. It is a tool designed for analysing and solving complex and interrelated dilemma using a network structure. Thus, the method is widely applied in numerous study fields, including healthcare, operations management, marketing, and most recently strategic management. It considers the interdependence among the studied criteria and focuses on the key relationships within the identified system (Liou et al., 2011). The DEMATEL method helps to understand a specific problem and evaluate possible solutions with a hierarchical structure. Different drivers of relocation strategy are expected to by related to one another both directly but also in a less obvious, indirect way. Therefore, DEMATEL can be used to first make the decision makers aware of the interdependencies, categorize the criteria that impact the reshoring-related decisions and eventually identify the improvement actions reducing the misinformation strain (Figure 5.3).

The research framework consists of three phases. The first phase focuses on identifying the key factors that influence reshoring-related decisions under geopolitical strain. These factors are derived from the literature and cross-referenced with experts' opinions. Experts were given a possibility to name other factors that, in their opinion, were relevant to the phenomenon but not included in the initial list, however no additional antecedents were provided. Data collection can be conducted either using the Delphi method (to reach consensus) or through questionnaires, (with the data ultimately being averaged). Here, the data was gathered using the Computer-Assisted Web Interviewing (CAWI) method, in which experts were asked to provide insights on two key areas: first, the factors contributing to the decision-making process on reshoring under geopolitical distortion, and second, the interrelationships among these factors. A total of 40 valid responses were obtained. All participants were management-level professionals working in manufacturing companies with over 15 years of experience, actively involved in decision-making related

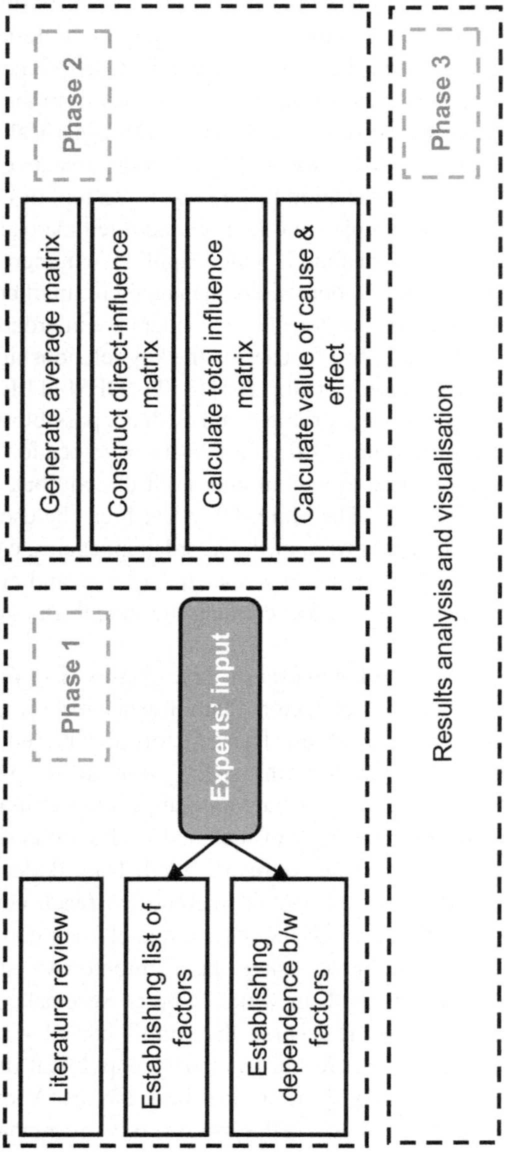

Figure 5.3 Research framework.

Source: Own elaboration.

to relocation (Table 5.2). The information they provided focused on the drivers of reshoring under geopolitical pressure. Data collection took place between November 2024 and February 2025.

Once the data is gathered, the first step of Phase 2 of the method is to prepare the initial direct relation matrix. The matrix encompasses the input from the experts who – based on pairwise comparison – indicate whether and to what degree an influence can be observed between factors. The evaluation is made with use of Likert scale where 0 stands for no influence, 1 for low influence, 2 for medium influence, 3 for high influence, and 4 for very high influence. The influence of factor A on factor B is denoted as x_{ij}. The diagonal elements of the matrix are depicted as 0. A separate non-negative matrix $n \times n$ is constructed for each expert which makes for a total number of 40 matrixes translated into initial direct relation matrix $A=[a_{ij}]$ using equation (1).

$$a_{ij} = \frac{1}{N}\sum_{k=1}^{N} x_{ij}^{k} \tag{1}$$

where k= the number of an expert evaluating the criteria,

Table 5.2 Overview of experts' characteristics

Characteristics		*N*	*%*
Current industry represented	Division 14 – Manufacture of wearing apparel	4	10.00
	Division 20 – Manufacture of chemicals and chemical products	7	17.50
	Division 21 – Manufacture of basic pharmaceutical products and pharmaceutical preparations	6	15.00
	Division 26 – Manufacture of computer, electronic, and optical products	8	20.00
	Division 28 – Manufacture of machinery and equipment n.e.c.	7	17.50
	Division 29 – Manufacture of motor vehicles, trailers, and semi-trailers	3	7.50
	Other manufacturing divisions	5	12.50
Age	Up to 20 years	28	70.00
	20 years and more	12	30.00

Source: Own elaboration.

N = total number of experts evaluating the criteria.

The matrix is then normalized (matrix D) using equation (2).

$$D = Z \text{ x } m$$

where

$$m = \left[\frac{1}{max_{1<i<n} \sum_{j=1}^{n} |a_{ij}|}, \frac{1}{max_{1<j<n} \sum_{i=1}^{n} |a_{ij}|} \right] \tag{2}$$

All elements of normalized matrix are between 0 and 1.

The normalized matrix will next be applied to calculate the total relation matrix defined as $W = D(I - D)^{-1}$, where I stands for identity matrix. The vectors r (3) and d (4) can now be derived from the matrix to depict the sum of direct and indirect influences of factor *i* on another factor and the total direct and indirect effect that other factors exert on factor *j*, respectively:

$$r = [r_i]_{nx1} = \left[\sum_{j=1}^{n} w_{ij} \right]_{nx1} \tag{3}$$

$$d = [d_j]_{nx1} = \left[\sum_{i=1}^{n} w_{ij} \right]_{1xn} \tag{4}$$

More explicitly, the sum of r_i and d_i ($r_i + d_i$) will represent the importance of a given factor in the network itself. Likewise, by deducting d_i from r_i ($r_i - d_i$) we calculate the net effect factor *i* brings into the network. Hence, if $r_i - d_i > 0$ we encounter a "net cause", whilst $r_i - d_i < 0$ depicts "net effect". Finally diagraph mapping the network of the relations can be prepared. To cover only the meaningful values and omit the negligible effect, the threshold value needs to be established. Here, the average of the elements in matrix W is used. In the last phase, the diagraph is prepared by generating 2-dimensional graph pinpointing the factors and their relations on ($r_i + d_i$, $r_i - d_i$) axes.

Delineating the factors influencing the reshoring-related decisions

Although the literature on reshoring is extensive, it remains highly fragmented. Pedroletti and Ciabuschi (2023) have conducted one of the most throughout and detailed systematic reviews on the reshoring process, covering its antecedents, decision-making, implementation, and outcome. However, their study, completed in 2022, does not account for major geopolitical developments. The authors themselves highlight this gap, emphasizing the need for further investigation of reshoring within the context of geopolitical contingencies. Therefore, to delineate the literature-based set of antecedents that might impact the reshoring process, we investigate papers that relate not only to geopolitics and reshoring but also more generally to trade and investment (Table 5.3).

Factors F1–F6 are directly linked to geopolitical developments and include disinformation in the investment country, cyberattacks in the investment country, the formation of (geo)political blocs, trade sanctions and transportation rearrangements. Disinformation can undermine trust in investors, who may struggle to distinguish between intentional misinformation and unintended miscommunication. As a result, uncertainty may increase, along with concerns over potential policy shifts. Similarly, cyberattacks can expose vulnerabilities in global supply chains, heightening fears over data security and operational continuity, which may drive reshoring. The formation of (geo)political blocs can reshape global trade dynamics, prompting companies to prioritize stability over expansive international reach. Meanwhile, trade sanctions can accelerate the regionalization of trade, making reshoring a crucial strategy. Sanctions, whether in the form of tariffs, non-tariff barriers, or outright trade bans, can disrupt company networks and force businesses to reconsider their supply chain strategies. Transportation bottlenecks have been visible since the COVID-19 pandemics but have since heightened due to geopolitical uncertainty, increasing the trade costs. Factors F7–F12 are not directly tied to geopolitical influences but have already been identified as reshoring antecedents in previous studies (Pedroletti & Ciabuschi, 2023). However, they may still play a significant role under geopolitical strain. Their indirect impact on other reshoring drivers could amplify their overall effect on the reshoring process.

Table 5.3 Literature-based and expert-based antecedents triggering reshoring under geopolitical disruptions

No.	*Name of factor*	*Explanation*	*Literature source*
F1	Disinformation in the investment country	Deliberate spread of false or misleading information within a country where an investment is being made or considered	(Mroczek-Dąbrowska, Cherubin, et al., 2024)
F2	Cyberattacks in the investment country	Deliberate and malicious efforts to breach, damage, or disrupt the digital infrastructure, networks, or systems of a country where an investment is being made or considered	(Mroczek-Dąbrowska, Cherubin, et al., 2024; Sahoo et al., 2024)
F3	Formation of (geo)political blocs	Creation of alliances or groupings of countries, regions, or political entities that align themselves based on shared geopolitical, economic, or strategic interests	(Kazancoglu et al., 2024)
F4	Trade sanctions	Punitive measures imposed by one or more countries on another country, group, or entity to influence behaviour, typically in response to actions considered hostile, illegal, or violating international law	(Klarin & Sosnovskikh, 2024; Weber & Stępień, 2020)
F5	Changes in transportation organization	Structural changes within a transportation system where the flow of goods, services, or people is slowed or restricted, often due to capacity limitations, inefficiencies, or disruption	(Ciriminna et al., 2024)
F6	Policy supporting the relocation of investments	Government actions, regulations, and incentives designed to encourage businesses or investors to move their operations, capital, or production activities from one location to another	(Di Stefano et al., 2024; Freund et al., 2024; Zeng & Kim, 2024)
F7	Uncertainty related to the election cycle	Instability or unpredictability that businesses or investors may experience due to political elections and their potential outcomes	(Ferriani et al., 2025)

Table 5.3 (Continued)

No.	*Name of factor*	*Explanation*	*Literature source*
F8	Industry 4.0 tools	Advanced technologies and digital solutions that are part of the fourth industrial revolution, which focuses on the integration of automation, data exchange, and smart technologies into manufacturing and other industrial sectors	(Dachs et al., 2019; Pegoraro et al., 2022)
F9	Bandwagon effect	Psychological phenomenon where people tend to adopt certain behaviours, beliefs, or opinions simply because they perceive that others are doing the same	(Barbieri et al., 2018)
F10	Changes in demand for offered products	Structural, permanent changes in the quantity of a product or service that consumers are willing and able to purchase in the investment market	(Grappi et al., 2018)
F11	Control	Desire, ability or power to better influence, manage, or regulate actions, processes, or outcomes of the investment when reshored	(Pegoraro et al., 2022; Robinson & Hsieh, 2016)
F12	Changes in wage costs at the investment location	Fluctuations in the average compensation paid to workers in a specific region or country where an investment is made or considered	(Barbieri et al., 2020)

Source: Own elaboration.

Data analysis and results

The analysis of the collected data adhered to the steps and procedures outlined in the "Methods, Data Collection, and Sample" subchapter. Given that DEMATEL was used to examine the interdependence among the factors and their influence on the reshoring phenomenon under geopolitical strain, we first removed factors considered irrelevant based on expert input. The experts indicated that the potential spread of disinformation was not considered significant to the reshoring process. Likewise, the impact of election cycles was deemed to have minimal relevance.

First the averaged matrix including the experts' input was generated using Eq. (1) and subsequently normalized using the Eq. (2). The normalized matrix is presented in Table 5.4.

Next, from the normalized direct-influence matrix, the total influence matrix was calculated (Table 5.5). The matrix depicts both direct and indirect influence the factors exert on one another. Based on the total influence matrix, factors that are the most influential (have the highest total influence) and factors that are more dependent (receive the most influence) were identified (with Eq. (3) and (4); Table 5.6).

The analysis presents interdependencies among ten factors assessed by experts as crucial antecedents affecting reshoring decisions. By evaluating these interactions, we can identify the most influential drivers, dependencies, and the overall structural patterns of the model. Based on the values of total influence matrix (Table 5.5) the threshold value (0.115) was calculated in order to identify the most critical relationships in the decision-support system and to construct an impact relationship map (Figure 5.4). The primary objective of the mapping is to determine key influencing factors, highly dependent factors, and feedback loops.

Key influencing factors are those that have strong outgoing relationships with others, thus they act as drivers in the network. The formation of geopolitical blocs emerges as a critical influencing

Table 5.4 The normalized direct-influence matrix

	F2	*F3*	*F4*	*F5*	*F6*	*F8*	*F9*	*F10*	*F11*	*F12*
F2	0.00	0.01	0.01	0.02	0.03	0.09	0.12	0.03	0.13	0.06
F3	0.04	0.00	0.14	0.15	0.15	0.01	0.05	0.09	0.06	0.03
F4	0.02	0.10	0.00	0.05	0.14	0.01	0.09	0.15	0.09	0.12
F5	0.01	0.01	0.03	0.00	0.02	0.00	0.12	0.15	0.10	0.14
F6	0.00	0.03	0.03	0.04	0.00	0.03	0.12	0.08	0.05	0.12
F8	0.11	0.00	0.00	0.04	0.00	0.00	0.02	0.04	0.10	0.17
F9	0.00	0.00	0.01	0.07	0.04	0.11	0.00	0.15	0.11	0.09
F10	0.00	0.00	0.00	0.07	0.01	0.10	0.00	0.00	0.07	0.17
F11	0.03	0.00	0.00	0.01	0.01	0.09	0.11	0.12	0.00	0.08
F12	0.00	0.00	0.00	0.00	0.02	0.11	0.12	0.11	0.08	0.00

Source: Own elaboration.

Table 5.5 Total influence matrix

	F2	*F3*	*F4*	*F5*	*F6*	*F8*	*F9*	*F10*	*F11*	*F12*
F2	0.03	0.02	0.02	0.07	0.05	0.17	0.19	0.13	0.21	0.17
F3	0.07	0.03	0.17	0.21	0.20	0.11	0.17	0.24	0.18	0.20
F4	0.05	0.11	0.03	0.13	0.19	0.13	0.21	0.30	0.21	0.29
F5	0.03	0.02	0.05	0.05	0.05	0.11	0.20	0.26	0.19	0.26
F6	0.02	0.04	0.04	0.08	0.03	0.12	0.19	0.18	0.14	0.23
F8	0.13	0.00	0.01	0.07	0.03	0.09	0.11	0.13	0.18	0.26
F9	0.03	0.01	0.02	0.12	0.06	0.19	0.08	0.25	0.20	0.22
F10	0.02	0.00	0.01	0.10	0.03	0.17	0.07	0.08	0.14	0.25
F11	0.05	0.00	0.01	0.05	0.03	0.17	0.16	0.20	0.08	0.18
F12	0.03	0.00	0.01	0.04	0.04	0.18	0.17	0.19	0.16	0.11

Source: Own elaboration.

Table 5.6 Cause-effect analysis of DEMATEL

Factor	*Ri*	*Ci*	*Ri+Ci*	*Ri-Ci*	*Relationship*
F2	1.072	0.456	1.528	0.616	Cause
F3	1.584	0.238	1.822	1.346	Cause
F4	1.646	0.358	2.005	1.288	Cause
F5	1.215	0.913	2.128	0.301	Cause
F6	1.072	0.710	1.782	0.362	Cause
F8	1.000	1.440	2.440	-0.440	Effect
F9	1.177	1.556	2.733	-0.379	Effect
F10	0.887	1.973	2.861	-1.086	Effect
F11	0.930	1.696	2.626	-0.766	Effect
F12	0.920	2.163	3.083	-1.243	Effect

Source: Own elaboration.

factor. It significantly impacts other elements of the model, like trade sanctions, changes in transportation organization, policy support, Industry 4.0 tools, bandwagon effect, changes in demand, control, and wage costs. The high outgoing influence suggests that shifts in global alliances and political realignments is driving the reshoring decision. Companies are likely to respond by reshoring operations to mitigate risks associated with growing geopolitical uncertainty and hostile sentiments. Trade sanctions act as another major influencer in the system. It strongly impacts policy support, technological development, bandwagon effect, changes in demand, control, and wage

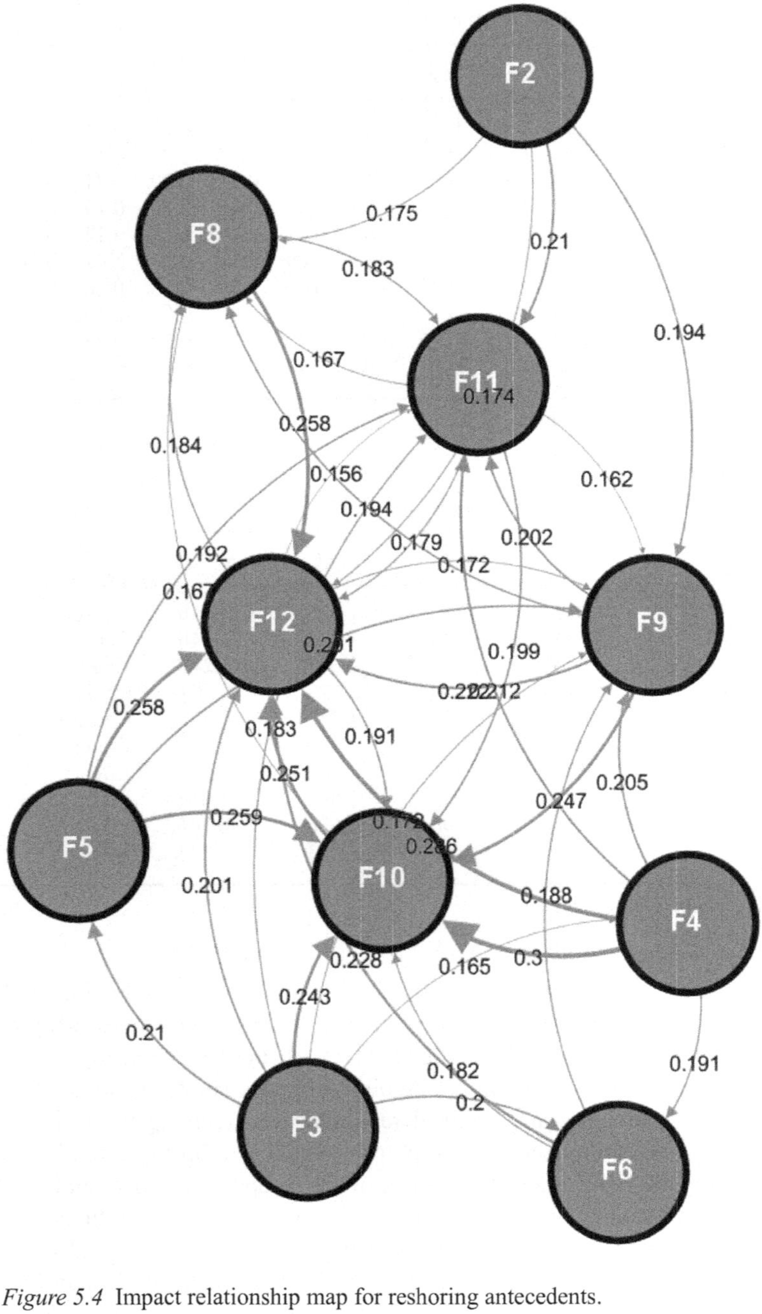

Figure 5.4 Impact relationship map for reshoring antecedents.

costs. Sanctions lead to economic isolation, prompting businesses to relocate production to avoid restrictive measures. A strong correlation with demand changes suggests that restricted trade alters consumer behaviour, further influencing investment decisions. Changes in transportation organization influence the bandwagon effect, demand changes, control, and wage costs. Disruptions in global logistics due to geopolitical tensions, conflicts, or regulatory shifts lead companies to reconsider previous offshore strategies.

Dependent factors have strong incoming influences, meaning they are shaped by other variables rather than influencing them. Changes in demand for offered products is the most highly dependent factor in the system, influenced by trade sanctions, formation of geopolitical blocs, transportation changes, and policy support. Changes in consumer demand are driven by policy shifts, trade restrictions, and technological developments. The Russian invasion of Ukraine demonstrated how demand for products and services, particularly in B2C markets, can be swiftly influenced by prevailing public sentiment towards the investor's country of origin. Changes in wage costs in the investment location are influenced by trade sanctions, formation of geopolitical blocs, policy support, transportation disruptions, and the bandwagon effect. Wage costs play a crucial role in relocation decisions during geopolitical tensions, but they typically serve as a long-term factor in the reshoring process, as evidenced by the case of China. Sanctions and industrial policies contribute to fluctuations in labour costs, affecting cost-based competitiveness in investment locations. Control is strongly influenced by cyberattacks, geopolitical blocs, trade sanctions, transportation disruptions, and the bandwagon effect. This takeaway is in line with the ongoing debate on the increasing managerial concern on security, operational continuity, and governance in overseas investments. Companies aim to regain control over supply chains, data security, and production processes amid global uncertainty.

Some factors show strong bidirectional relationships, indicating feedback loops where one factor reinforces the other. Such loops can be mostly seen among the "effect" factors, especially in relationship with the changes in wages in the investment country as well as the bandwagon effect and control. Rising labour costs may push companies to relocate the operations but it can often be the friendshoring or nearshoring rather a typical reshoring strategy. The bandwagon effect and demand changes reinforce each other, as the tendency of firms to follow competitors in reshoring decisions creates cascading effects. If major industry players relocate, suppliers and partners may follow.

An interesting takeaway is the fact that the antecedents F2–F5, which can be classified as "geopolitical factors" all belong to the causes (i.e. drivers) of the reshoring process, whilst the following factors, already seen in literature as unrelated to geopolitically-triggered relocation are dependant ones. In effect, it can be concluded that the geopolitical-related antecedents, like sanctions and formation of geopolitical blocs, transportation disruptions and cyberattacks are the triggers without which reshoring would not take place whilst the market-related factors are second-tier factors that do contribute to the process but do not drive the phenomenon.

Shifts in the antecedents of geopolitically driven reshoring?

The literature highlights that a key group of factors driving reshoring is the rise in various costs; these include labour costs, transportation expenses, environmental taxes, and others. Rising labour costs in emerging economies are slowly but visibly narrowing the wage gap which was one of the primary cost advantages of offshoring in the first place (Gray et al., 2017; Piatanesi & Arauzo-Carod, 2019). Various sources, including the World Bank Poverty and Inequality Platform indicate that both the median income and daily consumption have significantly increased in many traditional offshoring locations since 2010. For instance, the median income more than doubled in case of China and rose by approximately 50% in Vietnam, Indonesia or Bangladesh (D'Ambrosio & Lavoratori, 2025). The significance of these factors was also revealed in this study. Labour costs were closely interconnected with nearly all other factors and proved highly sensitive to changes among those antecedents. At the same time, fluctuations in labour costs had a direct impact on control and technology adoption, particularly in process automation.

The literature review points also to rise and development of automation and Industry 4.0 tools as drivers of reshoring initiatives. The general thesis assumes that with the application of technological enablers (e.g. robots, additive manufacturing, etc.) in home countries, companies will be able to replace foreign labour and in effect reduce marginal costs and enhance productivity. Again, Antràs (2020) claims that automation increases fixed domestic costs but can significantly lower marginal production costs, potentially driving relocation, especially in light of rising foreign costs. These findings were supported by Krenz et al. (2021) who directly link robotization with 3.5% increase in reshoring due to efficiency reasons. Likewise, the study at hand confirms that adoption of Industry 4.0 solutions in companies both drives reshoring and impact the labour cost structure.

Another group of factors driving reshoring is linked to deglobalization trends and broadly defined geopolitical tensions. These antecedents commonly include sanctions, tariff and non-tariff measures, policies and regulations promoting the return of capital, hybrid warfare, and the formation of economic and military blocs (Conteduca et al., 2025). While there is a strong belief in the importance of these factors, empirical evidence supporting their actual impact remains limited. The conducted study shows that the geopolitics-related factors not only trigger the reshoring under current events but also drive the process impacting the other factors in the network. However, there is still no consensus on how information distortion and hybrid warfare influence relocation strategies. While companies often name cyberattacks as the relocation driver, they frequently remain unaware of their vulnerability to disinformation spread.

Literature suggests that the rising costs of production, increasing uncertainty, and technological advancements should widespread reshoring. Yet, offshoring activities required specific investments, including market analysis, network establishment, infrastructure investments, and other costs which are largely sunk, meaning they cannot be easily recovered or redeployed elsewhere (Martin et al., 2023). Hence, unless a significant event leading to the loss of competitiveness abroad occurs, firms are likely to maintain the status quo. This phenomenon has been labelled the "stickiness of GVC" and reflects the durable nature of existing international production networks (Arte & Larimo, 2019). Reshoring would most likely require companies to incur similar sunk costs while relocating therefore paradoxically higher offshoring costs can anchor the existing investments. However, the impact of sunk costs also depends on the expected duration of external shocks. If cost increases are seen as temporary, firms may delay reshoring (e.g. COVID-19 pandemic, largely perceived as a short-term disruption, did not trigger widespread reshoring). However, if shocks are expected to persist, reshoring becomes justifiable. This has been often the case of geopolitical disruptions which are now viewed as a structural rather than cyclical occurrence.

6 International production trajectories under geopolitical strain

The case of semiconductors and wire harness systems

A chip, also known as integrated circuit or a semiconductor, is nothing else than "a small piece of semiconducting material (…) with millions or billions of microscopic transistors carved into it" (Miller, 2022, p. 15). Yet, the access to the chips has become an equivalent of national security as they power almost all and any of the technologies individuals, companies, or institutions use daily. The industry dates back to 1950s U.S. but has quickly become an example of a truly globalized value chain. As Miller (2022) states, a typical chip would most probably come from a blueprint designed in UK by a Japanese-owned company, with aid of Israeli and American engineers; manufactured in Taiwan with use of precision tools delivered by either a Dutch, Japanese, or American supplier; packed and tested in Southeast Asia to eventually be shipped to China for assembly. Given the scarcity of suppliers and their market position bordering on monopolistic dominance, the existing semiconductors' global value chain (GVC) has evolved as a relatively most cost-efficient network.

The reliance of manufacturing industries on the chip availability is overwhelming. The automotive sector, in particular, has been significantly impacted by the pandemic-related semiconductor shortage and it is estimated that more than 11 million car were pulled from production in 2021 alone. Ongoing bottlenecks in the semiconductor industry have been driven by factors initially triggered by lockdowns and shipment disruptions during the pandemic, and have persisted due to increased demand, material shortages, high production costs, and labour challenges. The car manufacturers, like Toyota, BMW, Hyundai, or Volkswagen, were prompted to relocate some of the production from Asia to Europe. Likewise, automotive suppliers, were

DOI: 10.4324/9781003724803-6

also driven to restructure their manufacturing plants and relocate some of the production processes back to Europe.

This chapter will examine the decision-making process of an automotive industry supplier regarding its relocation from Asia. The company, which is heavily dependent on the semiconductor industry, has decided to move one of its factories back to either Europe, the U.S. or other Asian country in response to global challenges surrounding chip availability. The company faced a critical choice between reshoring, nearshoring, and friendshoring options. The chapter will explore the decision-making process from the company's perspective, presenting a decision model that helps evaluate and rank alternative locations based on their potential to reduce geopolitical risk.

Reshoring, nearshoring, or rightshoring? The genesis of relocation strategy of automotive industry supplier

Since the pandemic, the automotive industry, which is a flagship example of a truly globalized value chain, has been hit with various disruptions, including the geopolitical tensions. The situation seems to finally stabilize with the global car production reaching 75.5 million units in 2024. Yet, geographically, among the key regions, Europe, North America, and Japan saw the most significant declines in the production output. European car production fell by 4.6% to 14.4 million units, reflecting a supply-demand adjustment following a surge driven by backlogs in 2023. Car production in the EU dropped by 6.2%, as industry confidence remained considerably weaker than in other European manufacturing sectors (Economic and Market Report Global and EU auto industry: Full year 2024, 2025).

The EU's industry, however, is encountering several challenges that might lead to the automotive GVC's reconfiguration. Firstly, the European automotive sector's shift towards electric vehicles (EVs) is causing a major transformation in the supplier landscape, rendering traditional combustion engine suppliers less competitive (if not obsolete altogether) and creating demand for new types of suppliers. At the same time, policymakers are striving to reduce dependence on third-country suppliers, a difficult task given that some components and materials are only available from outside EU. This creates a trade-off between the EU's long-standing drive for free competition and the need to secure industry's resilience. The EU is pushing for shortening of the GVCs and making them more local, which means that the industry is also experiencing a rapid push towards automation and the implementation of Industry 4.0 technologies. In effect, we can observe consolidation and relocation strategies that alter the existing *status quo*. The technological advancements are further driven by the new regulations and standards which aim to reduce carbon footprints and other environmental burdens.

This chapter relates to a study in which the case of automotive industry supplier is discussed. The company[1] has been established in 1996 in Poland and manufactures wire harness systems that are primarily used for utility vehicles but can also be used for machinery and other transportation vessels. The Company has become part of a global multinational enterprise (MNE) with production sites in China, the U.S., and the EU.

Wire harness systems are a key part of any vehicle's electrical system. In specifics, they are a bundle of electrical wires, connectors, terminals, and other components that allow for transmitting electrical power and signals to various parts of the vehicle. Their function is to connect automotive components (e.g. engine, lights, sensors, audio systems) and facilitate communication between them. Traditional wire harness systems were not as dependent on the semiconductors as their contemporary counterparts. Chips are now used to control and manage power flow, data transmission, and other electronic functions of the wire harness systems. As a result, the company has become a prime example of operations that are, on one hand, highly vulnerable to geopolitical tensions and, on the other, subject to the concerns of EU's geoeconomics.

The Company's operations are susceptible to geopolitical risks. Following the rollout of the Russian invasion in Ukraine in 2022, the Company experienced some mild disruptions to its manufacturing processes across various locations, but especially in Europe. Initially, it faced temporary shortages of raw materials and significant price volatility. However, these issues did not lead to permanent delays in production timelines. The primary concern for the Company was related to shipping arrangements, but overall, the impact was not severe. However, the disruption itself made the company more aware of the geopolitical exposure of their globalized production chain. Following an internal audit, the Company identified looming geopolitical threats that were perceived as the most significant ones to the resilience of its operations. The major fear of the Company was the deterioration of China–Taiwan relations and what could follow – the disruption in the semiconductors' availability. The Company has already experienced the chips' shortages due to the COVID-19 pandemics and feared the re-emergence of the problem.

The China–Taiwan conflict has long been a source of geopolitical tension, however it was the Russian invasion of Ukraine in 2022 that served as a trigger, making the Company re-evaluate its international strategy and manufacturing value chain. As discussed by Caldara and Iacoviello (2022) it is often not the geopolitical act itself that impacts the company's strategies but the geopolitical threat that prompts the companies to adopt changes. The Company has decided to address the geopolitical challenges and relocate one of its manufacturing facilities from China to another location. The decision on how and where to relocate the plant was however a complex issue that will be examined in the subsequent sections of this chapter. The discussion is a two-part study that is based on the interviews with the company's representatives and the review of secondary materials (press releases and internal company documents) relating to the reshoring decision. The aim of the first part of the study is to verify whether the conceptual model of reshoring developed in Chapter 5 was applicable in the Company's case. Multiple ranking methods were employed to identify the most suitable location for reshoring the Company's operations. Second part of the study aims to discuss the actual decision of the company on the new plant location and mangers' perception of the validity and usefulness of the developed model.

Background

As mentioned before, the Company's manufacturing process and end-product are widely dependent on semiconductor's availability and supply chain continuity. The Company procured semiconductors from five different companies, however all components were delivered from Asia, specifically from Taiwan and South Korea. With the increase in semiconductor manufacturing capabilities in China (about 17% of the global production as of 2023), the Company has decided on major strategic pivot related to relocation.

The Company had several wire harness systems plants located in the U.S., Mexico, Canada, India, Poland, and China. The ones established in Canada, the U.S., and Mexico were relatively well secured as the company had plans for shifting at least part of the procurement process to the American suppliers. However other locations remained dependent on the Asian supplies. The Company was mostly apprehensive of the Chinese factory. On one hand, they considered either moving procurement to Chinese semiconductor manufacturers or relocating the manufacturing plant. The company was concerned that the escalating Chinese–Taiwan conflict could disrupt plant operations, or that the worsening of U.S.–China relations could place the Chinese manufacturing plant in a more vulnerable position as it had foreign ownership. Eventually, the Company decided to relocate the Chinese manufacturing plant and considered various locations in Europe and North America. The idea to shift the procurement process to Chinese suppliers was abandoned given that the company did not intend to increase its dependency on China (Figure 6.1).

Alternative locations – reshoring, nearshoring, or rightshoring?

After the initial location analysis the Company seriously considered three alternative reshoring locations: Mexico, Germany, and Türkiye.

Mexico was considered since the Company already had several subsidiaries in the country, one also in the wire harness systems sector. If the location was chosen, the existing plant would be expected to triple its capacity at that time. This might prove difficult (yet not unfeasible) since the existing location offered space constrains. However, the labour force was experienced and would require least up-skilling or re-skilling out of the three locations. The Company also hoped to benefit from the changes in procurement strategy for the chips, however as the shift for American sourcing was still underway, this was still treated as an unsure development. Choosing Mexico would however, in a way, limit the geographical footprint of the Company which still considered its operations to be global and feared regionalization.

Türkiye was considered as a new destination that had not been part of company's portfolio. The country's favourable geographical position facilitates access to both European and Middle Eastern markets. Türkiye's relatively well-developed infrastructure, including especially the transportation network, and proximity to major manufacturing hubs, simplifies shipment arrangements. However, as discussed in Chapter 2, ongoing disputes over access to certain routes remained a concern for the Company. Türkiye's skilled labor force and expertise in the automotive and electronics industries, which are key customers for the company, also made it an appealing option. While there were

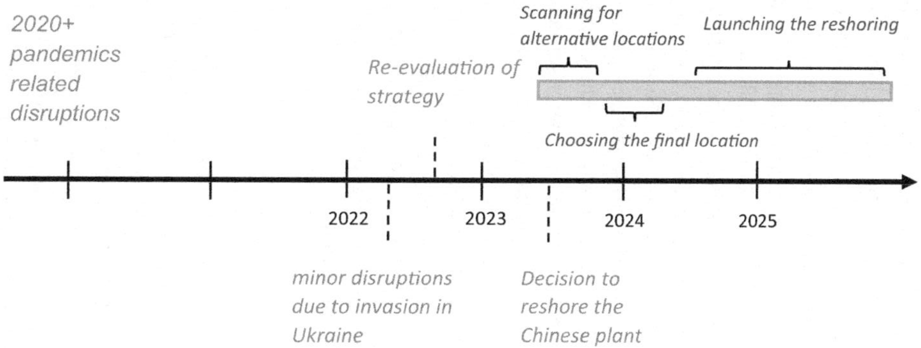

Figure 6.1 Timeline of the relocation-decision process (current and predicted).

Source: Own elaboration based on interviews and Company's internal materials.

also some government incentives for foreign investments, these were comparable to those offered by other locations. What was of interest to the Company was that Türkiye's stance in geopolitical disputes, particularly regarding China, can be generally described as a pragmatic and non-confrontational. While Türkiye maintains strong economic ties with China, especially through trade and infrastructure projects such as the Belt and Road Initiative, it has also established strong diplomatic relations with both China and other global powers.

The final option the Company considered was Germany, where it already maintained operations, though not within the wire harness systems sector. Germany is emerging as Europe's frontrunner in semiconductor manufacturing, driven by substantial subsidies and increased investment under the European Chips Act. The country is renowned for its highly skilled labour force, particularly in engineering, and boasts a deeply embedded industrial ecosystem. Numerous manufacturing firms – especially from the automotive sector – have established their headquarters or production facilities there. The Company anticipated potential synergies from the presence of major semiconductor players such as Intel and Taiwan Semiconductor Manufacturing Company (TSMC). Moreover, Germany's proximity to the Netherlands – widely recognized as a global leader in semiconductor equipment – was seen as a strategic advantage. In the context of increasing regionalization of value chains, this location was viewed as offering strong support and long-term potential, with similar advantages as Mexico but with keeping the operations more global.

Data collection

The Company was considering three alternative locations for reshoring its Chinese plant. For the purpose of this study top management of the Company was interviewed in a series of meetings (Table 6.1) to verify whether the model established in Chapter 5 would prove useful in determining the final relocation spot and to afterwards reference it to the actual decision that was made. The exercise was designed to delineate the limitations of the model, to compare decision and to analyse the significance of contextual, often subjective factors, on the decision process and the outcome itself. The single case study design has proven useful for studies on relocation strategies or nonlinear internationalization (Pedroletti, 2025; Vissak & Francioni, 2013).

Table 6.1 Interview's overview

Interviewees	*Function*	*Functional area*	*Seniority*	*Number of interviews*	*Evaluation of locations*
I1	Executive	General strategy	32	3	Yes
I2	Executive	General strategy	22	2	No
I3	Director	Manufacturing	5	1	Yes
I4	Manager	Market analysis	7	2	Yes
I5	Manager	Sales	11	1	No
I6	Manager	Procurement	4	3	Yes
I7	Manager	Manufacturing	15	2	No

Source: Own elaboration.

The data collected ranged from 2020 to 2025 and covered both retrospective interviews as well as current and forecasted developments. A total of 14 in-depth and semi-structured interviews were conducted with 7 managers of the Company. Interviewees were initially selected based on their involvement in the reshoring process, with four key informants identified by the researcher. The remaining three participants were recommended by senior management, who pinpointed additional employees capable of providing deeper insights into the decision-making process. The interviewees differed in seniority which enabled the study to capture both strategic perception of the Company and its overall fit for the investment portfolio as well as operational perspective which included insights into procurement and manufacturing steps. The interviews were primarily conducted online, with only a few sessions held in person. On average, each session lasted 45 minutes and was conducted either in Polish or English, depending on the respondent's origin. All interviews were recorded and transcribed verbatim with the exception of the meetings where evaluation exercise took place. These meetings resulted in written output that was delivered by the respondents in an electronic form. The data collected was cross-referenced with both internal documents shared by the Company and available media releases. Since the functional area of interviewees differed and so did their perspectives on the process, this enabled the researcher to verify the accuracy of the information and alleviate some of the "recall bias". The complementary materials, including internal documents, archival data, and media reports amounted to about 100 pages relating to both locations and the decision-making process.

Comparative analysis of MCDM methods for ranking Company's relocation choices

The model developed in Chapter 5 conceptualizes the antecedents that drive the relocation process. At the same time, it serves as a framework for assessing whether the post-relocation site exhibits similar challenges or demonstrates relative stability. Accordingly, the same set of drivers is considered here, but they are applied to evaluate the robustness of the newly selected alternative. If the new location does not manifest issues associated with these antecedents, the Company is less likely to encounter comparable pressures or contemplate another relocation in the foreseeable future.

The initial interviews were dedicated to understanding the challenges the company faced, the unique circumstances relating to the reshoring decision and specificity of the manufacturing process, including the supply chain dependencies. Once the backbone of the study was established, the interviews turned to process of location selection which included assessing the relocation model's applicability to the Company. A series of meetings were arranged where the respondents, representing different functional areas discussed the model and its elements. Once all clarifications were addressed, the interviewees were tasked with evaluating three alternative locations the company considered against the criteria used in the model. Their responses were then used to rank the locations according to different weighting methods from multicriteria decision-making analysis.

The weights can be established as both objective and subjective components. Both approaches have their merits; subjective weight are derived from expert opinions and incorporate specific managerial judgments relating to a specific case whereas the objective weights stem from actual data of the alternatives and hence are not burdened by the respondents' biases (Lee & Chang, 2018). This study deploys both subjective and objective weighting to make a comparison between the ranking alternatives and how they impact the outcome of the analysis.

Since weight establishment is a crucial step in Multi-Criteria Decision Making (MCDM), the study compares three approaches: the Analytic Hierarchy Process (AHP), the Shannon's Entropy and the Gini's method

(Table 6.2). The AHP methods is a subjective one as it relies on pair-wise comparisons of criteria based on expert judgment. It is valued for its structured approach and ability to incorporate managerial insights but at the same time can be biased if the data is inconsistent. The study applied Krippendorff's alpha (Hughes, 2024) as a statistical measure assessing the reliability of agreement among responders. The value amounted to 0.78 which allows to conclude that the data is reliable. On the other hand, the Shannon's Entropy is an objective technique that assigns weights based on the degree of information diversity within the decision matrix. This method is purely data-driven, in contrast to the AHP method. It makes it more objective but at the same time it can forego any contextual dependence that cannot be captured by statistics itself. The final method, the Gini's approach measures inequality or dispersion within a dataset. It assigns greater weight to criteria with more inequality, interpreting them as more influential in distinguishing between alternatives. It is also an objective weighting approach.

Table 6.2 Weighting scenarios with AHP, Shannon's entropy, and Gini's methods

No.	*Name of factor*	*AHP*	*Shannon's Entropy*	*Gini's method*
F2	Security against cyberattacks in the new host country	0.107	0.170	0.152
F3	Belonging to the (geo)political block of the investor	0.126	0.170	0.152
F4	Trade sanctions resilience of the new host country	0.111	0.024	0.050
F5	Beneficial transportation organization	0.096	0.024	0.050
F6	Policy supporting the relocation of investments in the new host country	0.101	0.005	0.024
F8	Degree of adoption of Industry 4.0 tools in the new host country	0.100	0.050	0.084
F9	Bandwagon effect toward new host country	0.089	0.065	0.095
F10	Changes in demand allocation after relocating to new host country	0.091	0.048	0.081
F11	Control over investment in the new host country	0.090	0.048	0.081
F12	Risk of changes in wage costs in the new host country	0.090	0.396	0.233

Source: Own elaboration.

The comparison of weights derived from AHP, Shannon's Entropy, and Gini's method reveals significant differences in how in each method the importance of various factors is interpreted. The AHP approach assigns relatively balanced weights across all factors, emphasizing trade sanctions and transportation changes more than the other two methods. Shannon's Entropy and Gini's method assign significantly higher weights to factors like cyberattacks, geopolitical blocs, and especially changes in wage costs, indicating that these factors show the greatest variability or inequality across the dataset. For instance, wage costs (F12) receive the highest weight under Entropy (0.396) and Gini (0.233), but only 0.090 in AHP, suggesting experts may undervalue its real-world differentiating power. In contrast, trade sanctions and transportation changes receive low weights under Entropy and Gini, implying consistent values across cases. These discrepancies highlight the value of integrating both subjective and objective methods to capture a more holistic view of factor significance.

Once the weights were established, the study turned to ranking the locations with the use of various MCDM methods. Four methods were chosen, namely the weighted sum method (WSM), Technique for Order Preference by Similarity to Ideal Solution (TOPSIS), VIseKriterijumska Optimizacija I Kompromisno Rešenje (VIKOR), and ÉLimination Et Choix Traduisant la REalité (ELECTRE). All these ranking techniques are widely recognized for their suitability to aid addressing the location decision problems (Saeidi et al., 2023; Yesilcayir et al., 2024). The WSM is relatively the simplest of the set, where scores are calculated by summing weighted normalized values; it is hence ideal for straightforward problems but shows limited applicability when trade-offs or non-linearities are involved. TOPSIS selects the option closest to the ideal solution and farthest from the worst, emphasizing geometric closeness, which suits problems where balance across criteria is assumed. VIKOR, on the other hand, introduces a compromise solution by considering both group utility and individual regret, making it useful when decision-makers seek a balanced trade-off. ELECTRE relies again on pairwise comparisons using concordance and discordance indices, making it more robust in handling qualitative data and in cases where full compensation between criteria is not acceptable. The study makes the comparison for all sets of weights established in previous step (Tables 6.3–6.6).

The ranking of the three reshoring locations – Germany, Mexico, and Türkiye – varied depending on both the MCDM method used and

Table 6.3 WSM ranking algorithm with differentiated weights

	AHP		*Shannon's Entropy*		*Gini's method*	
	Score	*Rank*	*Score*	*Rank*	*Score*	*Rank*
Türkiye	0.306	3	0.355	2	0.334	2
Germany	0.371	1	0.375	1	0.389	1
Mexico	0.324	2	0.270	3	0.308	3

Source: Own elaboration.

the weighting scheme applied (Table 6.7). With AHP weights applied, Germany ranked first across WSM and TOPSIS, while Türkiye emerged as the top location under VIKOR, reflecting its strength when compromise-based decision logic is applied. ELECTRE II, however, was non-conclusive, emphasizing the method's conservative nature and its sensitivity to discordance. When Shannon's Entropy was used (objective, variability-based weights), Germany maintained the top position in WSM and TOPSIS, but Mexico ranked first in VIKOR, showing how entropy's focus on informational content can shift preferences. With Gini-based weights, the pattern repeated: Germany dominated WSM and TOPSIS, while Mexico again took the lead under VIKOR. Interestingly, ELECTRE II only produced a conclusive ranking for Türkiye, placing it last under objective weights, while failing to rank the top two. Across all scenarios, Germany was most frequently ranked first, especially with subjective (AHP) and weighted-sum methods. Mexico's performance improved under objective methods, particularly in VIKOR, while Türkiye's rank was highly dependent on the method, performing best only under AHP-VIKOR. These differences highlight how both weight origin and method logic significantly influence MCDM ranking outcome.

In this specific case, we deal with a reversal in rankings between TOPSIS and VIKOR methods. This indicates differences in how these alternatives are being evaluated under each framework. While TOPSIS prioritizes alternatives closest to the ideal solution, VIKOR focuses on a compromise between group benefit and individual regret, in effect minimizing the worst-case outcome. Hence, a location that performs well on average but poorly in one key criterion may still rank highly in TOPSIS but be penalized in VIKOR. In case of the Company, this has been evident while evaluating the "risk of changes in wage costs in the

Table 6.4 TOPSIS ranking algorithm with differentiated weights

	AHP				*Shannon's Entropy*				*Gini's method*			
	Si+	*Si-*	*Ci*	*Rank*	*Si+*	*Si-*	*Ci*	*Rank*	*Si+*	*Si-*	*Ci*	*Rank*
Türkiye	0.08	0.03	0.25	3	0.07	0.16	0.71	2	0.08	0.06	0.44	2
Germany	0.01	0.08	0.84	1	0.04	0.11	0.72	1	0.02	0.09	0.84	1
Mexico	0.03	0.05	0.65	2	0.17	0.02	0.12	3	0.07	0.03	0.31	3

Source: Own elaboration.

Table 6.5 VIKOR ranking algorithm with differentiated weights

	AHP				*Shannon's Entropy*				*Gini's method*			
	Si	*Ri*	*Qi*	*Rank*	*Si*	*Ri*	*Qi*	*Rank*	*Si*	*Ri*	*Qi*	*Rank*
Türkiye	0.726	0.126	1.000	1	0.515	0.170	0.315	2	0.693	0.152	0.652	2
Germany	0.200	0.096	0.083	3	0.265	0.198	0.062	3	0.194	0.116	0.000	3
Mexico	0.399	0.090	0.189	2	0.662	0.396	1.000	1	0.552	0.233	0.858	1

Source: Own elaboration.

Table 6.6 ELECTRE II ranking algorithm with differentiated weights

	AHP				*Shannon's Entropy*				*Gini's method*			
	T	*G*	*M*	*Rank*	*T*	*G*	*M*	*Rank*	*T*	*G*	*M*	*Rank*
Türkiye	0	0	0	2-3	0	0	0	3	0	0	0	3
Germany	0	0	0	1–2–3	1	0	0	1–2	1	0	0	1–2
Mexico	1	0	0	1–2	1	0	0	1–2	1	0	0	1–2

Source: Own elaboration.

new host country" criteria. This divergence highlights this outlier in the data, especially when we consider Table 6.1 and disproportionate weight for F12. Such a reversal doesn't signal an error but emphasizes the importance of understanding the decision logic behind each method. It also suggests that decision-makers should look closely at criteria-level performance and weight sensitivity to choose a method that aligns best with their goals – whether it be optimal overall performance or a balanced compromise. In summary, according to the model, the Company should relocate its operations to Germany if they were searching for the overall best location and to Mexico if they were searching for a second-best option that would leverage all criteria.

Managerial insights on the decision-making process

The application of the research model allowed for fairly objective selection of the reshoring location, pointing to two choices – Germany or Mexico, depending on the strategy of the Company. The following section will be dedicated to cross-comparison of the actual reshoring decision and decision-making process with the empirical model. The aim of the analysis is twofold: first, to identify the differences between a purely data-driven decision-making approach and a managerial approach in the selection process; and second, to highlight the contextual factors influencing the decision that cannot be captured by the model.

The executive team leading the reshoring effort spent approximately six months selecting three previously mentioned locations – Mexico, Germany, and Türkiye – each offering distinct advantages. This was followed by nearly a year of debate before reaching a final

Table 6.7 Summary of location's ranking according to weights and methods

Rank	*AHP*				*Shannon's Entropy*				*Gini's method*			
	WSM	*TOPSIS*	*VIKOR*	*ELECTREII*	*WSM*	*TOPSIS*	*VIKOR*	*ELECTREII*	*WSM*	*TOPSIS*	*VIKOR*	*ELECTREII*
1	Germany	Germany	Türkiye	Non-conclusive	Germany	Germany	Mexico	Non-conclusive	Germany	Germany	Mexico	Non-conclusive
2	Mexico	Mexico	Mexico	Non-conclusive	Mexico	Türkiye	Türkiye	Non-conclusive	Türkiye	Türkiye	Türkiye	Non-conclusive
3	Türkiye	Türkiye	Germany	Non-conclusive	Türkiye	Mexico	Germany	Türkiye	Mexico	Mexico	Germany	Türkiye

Source: Own elaboration.

decision. The final choice was indeed made between Mexico and Germany. Both locations had merits, but several time-specific factors ultimately favoured the European site.

The decision process

While making its decision, the Company considered three key groups of factors: geopolitical conditions, cost efficiency, and market access. These groups were not broken down to individual factors but were treated as elements of financial forecasts prepared for each investment site. Among geopolitical factors, the Company prepared scenarios assuming trade restrictions (tariff barriers), surge in logistical costs due to procurement challenges and any potential subsidies or reliefs offered by the host country. The cost factors included any costs related to launching the operations and upholding them, including scenarios that assumed an increase in sustainability-related requirements (especially in Germany). The market access factors were most challenging to incorporate, as the Company did not have a clear understanding to what degree the relocation would impact their sales ability. The financial forecasts were the reference point for further discussions and decision-making. They were not decisive in final selection but they already indicated that Türkiye would most probably be the least cost-effective option.

The global footprint

As mentioned before the Company has global presence and maintains its operations in vehicle electrification and connectivity solutions on a global scale. It means that it both sales these solutions worldwide (either through its own distribution network and sales representations) and that it owns manufacturing sites and brands in various countries in Asia, Europe, and America. Considering the geopolitical outlook, the Company feared potential retaliation towards its Chinese subsidiary, if the relationship between the U.S. and China deteriorated. However, relocating the Chinese plant had a major impact on the company's structure, as finalizing the reshoring process meant that, in Asia, the Company would only be left with a factory in India.

One of the key factors that the Company considered in its location selection process was the investment portfolio. Even though the procurement of semiconductors was more reliable if the operations were reshored to Mexico, the Company feared losing its "global" footprint if too many processes were regionalized. While proximity to the U.S. headquarters offered logistical advantages, over-reliance on a single regional hub may have reduced the global outreach.

> *We were already scaling up in both Mexico and the U.S., in other type of industries but we were growing there. We feared that bringing too much back [to the region] would eventually mean, we became a regional and not global company.*
>
> *(Interviewee 1)*

The bandwagon effect

The wire harness manufacturing industry in China is characterized by weak concentration, with over 5,500 registered manufacturers – most of which are domestically owned. While a few global players have established manufacturing facilities in the country, particularly in Eastern China, they represent a small share of the market. Since 2019, many companies have pursued consolidation as a key strategy, given that other growth pathways have become increasingly limited.

The foreign-owned companies in China have however started to turn to reshoring strategies more visibly. For instance, one of the Company's main competitors, who also manufactures wire harness systems particularly for the automotive, marine, and industrial sectors has reshored one of its four manufacturing plants to Germany. The competitor has reshored both manufacturing processes and R&D operations to Europe. Other foreign-owned companies follow suit, either pursuing typical backshoring or adopting dual manufacturing model.

The Company has been diligently monitoring its competitors, especially other foreign-owned ones, as to their strategy and reshoring locations. Europe, specifically Germany, Hungary, and Czechia have been frequently targeted as the new investment sites. This trend has significantly influenced the Company's own decision-making, reinforcing the strategic appeal of a German location, especially since its competitors have started to engage in joint collaborations on developing new solutions in semiconductor technology. The Company secured a similar partnership, and the initiative was scheduled to be launched in mid-2025, aligned with the planned relocation of part of its operations.

> *Germany has become a strategic hub for chips, and if we want to stay on top, we need to be part of that ecosystem. Our competitors are already forging alliances. We simply can't afford to be on the sidelines.*
>
> *(Interviewee 4)*

Market penetration

An important consideration was the strategic role of the Chinese subsidiary within the Company's global network. The relocation implied that the markets previously served by this facility would either need to be abandoned or supplied through alternative arrangements. The Company acknowledged that preserving full market coverage was unattainable; however, it aimed to maintain approximately 65–70% of its original operations. The shift in production location necessitated adjustments to logistics frameworks, trade procedures, and related operational structures. The Chinese plant had historically supported both Asian and European markets, which rendered relocation to the U.S. particularly impractical. This option was constrained by prohibitive transportation costs and heightened uncertainty surrounding trade regulations under the Trump administration, which made export activities unpredictable. Consequently, Türkiye and Germany emerged as more viable alternatives.

From a theoretical standpoint, Germany appeared preferable due to stable trade relations within the European Union and the absence of significant reshoring policies, which suggested continuity in operations and sales. Nevertheless, access to Asian markets could become increasingly restricted in light of unpredictable geopolitical developments. In the long term, the Company intended to reorient its sales strategy toward a stronger European focus, which further reinforced the attractiveness of Germany as a relocation destination.

The comparison of approaches

As previously noted, the final decision was to reshore operations to Germany. The contextual factors discussed herein supported this outcome, and although they were not incorporated into the original model, they proved to be significant. According to the Company's management, beyond geopolitical considerations, the most influential elements were the bandwagon effect and the firm's global orientation.

In reviewing the comparative analysis of Mexico and Germany, the Company emphasized that its optimization objective was not to satisfy all criteria simultaneously but rather to identify the location that would maximize overall benefits, given the unpredictability of certain variables.

Management further underscored that, for the model to be effectively integrated into formal decision-making processes, the organizational unit must possess a clear understanding of its strategic intent and optimization priorities – an endeavour that is often challenging within complex corporate ecosystems. Additionally, the Company indicated that it perceives the model primarily as a screening instrument rather than a definitive decision-making framework, as firm-specific factors are difficult to capture through a generalized approach. Nevertheless, the exercise was acknowledged as a valuable confirmatory tool that introduced an element of objectivity into the decision-making process.

Note

1 At the company's request, the firm's name has been anonymized.

7 Policy frameworks for reshoring in CEE

A review of the existing solutions and EU expectations

Although the implementation of the industrial policy and other regulations aimed at assisting national development and resilience building is controversial at best, more and more governments make use of it. Industrial policy can be defined as governmental involvement in forms of job protection, grants, loans, tax incentives, or other interventions expected to foster industrial development, technological advancements, and structural transformation (Johnstone & Kivimaa, 2018). The industrial policy is meant to target specific industries or sectors that are of significant importance. Often these are manufacturing industries, high-tech industries and energy sector. The regulations are often accompanied with specific trade policies including protective measures like tariffs, quotas, or trade restrictions to shield domestic industries from foreign competition (Curran et al., 2021).

This chapter focuses on an overview of existing policies and regulations in the European Union (EU) that directly impact the reconfiguration of global value chains (GVCs). On one hand, the discussion relates to some industry specific policies, such as the semiconductors. On the other hand, it discusses the impact of the megatrends on EU's approach to industrial policy. The chapter also considers how the geopolitical disruptions are likely to impact Europe's regulatory attempts towards reshoring.

EU's industrial policy? On a lookout for changes

Traditionally, the EU has favoured supporting research and innovation rather than implementing industrial policy tools. Such approach ensured maintenance of market competitiveness and single market

DOI: 10.4324/9781003724803-7

integrity. Yet, with the increasing geopolitical tensions, the EU has been forced to balance its historical openness with securing autonomy in some crucial sectors (Curran & Joltreau, 2024). So far, the principle that Member States with greater resources should not be allowed to outcompete weaker ones by subsidizing entire sectors of their national economy prevailed. The only exception, until the European Chips Act of February 2022, has been the EU's regional policy that allowed the less developed regions to seek State aid for industrial production projects (Duchâtel, 2022).

The rollout of the EU–China trade has however prompted EU to reconsider its approach to industrial policy and governmental intervention. EU finds itself at a disadvantage to control the ever-growing trade and investment imbalances and has developed a set of "autonomous defensive tools" which include specific trade instruments. The overall aim is to, similarly to U.S., regulate technology transfers abroad, especially to China. The adopted policies do not however intend to cut off all international ties, as creating self-sufficiency of the EU is simply not a reachable goal (Duchâtel, 2022). The pragmatic approach is however to create regulations and incentives that would reduce EU's vulnerabilities and build resilience capacity.

Existing EU legal frameworks – originally designed for market integration – are increasingly being repurposed to enable the emergence of industrial policies. Internal market provisions, particularly Article 114 Treaty on the Functioning of the European Union (TFEU), have become a key legal basis for harmonization measures that indirectly advance industrial objectives (Dermine & Patrin, 2026). Recent initiatives such as the Net Zero Industry Act, the European Chips Act, and the Critical Raw Materials Act (CRM Act) illustrate how internal market regulation is "converted" into a tool for strengthening strategic sectors and ensuring resilience. Similarly, state aid rules, traditionally restrictive, have undergone significant flexibilization (De Witte, 2025). The Commission's Temporary Crisis and Transition Framework and relaxed criteria for Important Projects of Common European Interest (IPCEI) allow targeted subsidies for green technologies and strategic industries, mitigating competitive distortions while fostering innovation. Budgetary instruments complement these efforts: programs like Horizon Europe and InvestEU, alongside transformative mechanisms such as NextGenerationEU and the Recovery and Resilience Facility, have endowed the EU with fiscal capacity to finance industrial priorities. Economic governance and cohesion policy further reinforce this trend (Wigger, 2023). Through the European Semester, the EU co-directs national reforms and investments, increasingly linking fiscal flexibility to commitments in green and digital transitions. Cohesion policy, traditionally focused on regional convergence, now integrates industrial concerns via Smart Specialization Strategies and channels substantial funding toward competitiveness and innovation. Collectively, these frameworks create enabling conditions for industrial policy without formal Treaty revision, demonstrating how second-order legal resources can be strategically mobilized to reconcile market integration with proactive economic intervention.

Regulating the industrial policy includes creating ecosystem in which reshoring strategic manufacturing back to Europe is not only feasible but also sustainable. The attempts have been visible since 2013 (e.g. Renaissance of Industry for a Sustainable Europe Strategy) and when the aim of reaching 20% share of manufacturing in the EU GDP was set. Yet, the declarations did not match the actions as very few initiatives actually addressed the reshoring incentives. The focus was still set on reaching technological sovereignty. One of the examples is the European Chips Act of 2022 which was intended to quadruple Europe's production of semiconductors and increase its global market share from 10% to 20% by 2030 through allocating 11 billion euro in the undertaking (Duchâtel, 2022). Simultaneously, private investments are given financial support by EU-related institutions to relocate. For comparison Figure 7.1's tracks the governmental interventions, including subsidies, in semiconductors, including integrated circuits and chips between 2021 and early 2025 (end of January).

The previously mentioned European Chips Act is one of the few initiatives that directly incentivizes reshoring. It was officially adopted by the European Parliament on 11 July 2023 and subsequently approved by the Council of the EU on 25 July 2023. It is similar to the U.S. Chips Act as both intend to boost domestic semiconductor manufacturing and, in effect, reduce reliance on foreign suppliers, especially the Asian ones (Table 7.1).

The European Chip Act is supposed to address the needs of the tech start-ups and SMEs that struggle with lack of funding. By setting grant system (including Horizon Europe) it aims to boost both design capacities of the industry and human resource shortages that require re- and up-skilling. At the same time, the Act is meant to support set-up of the so-called "mega-fabs", plants able to produce high

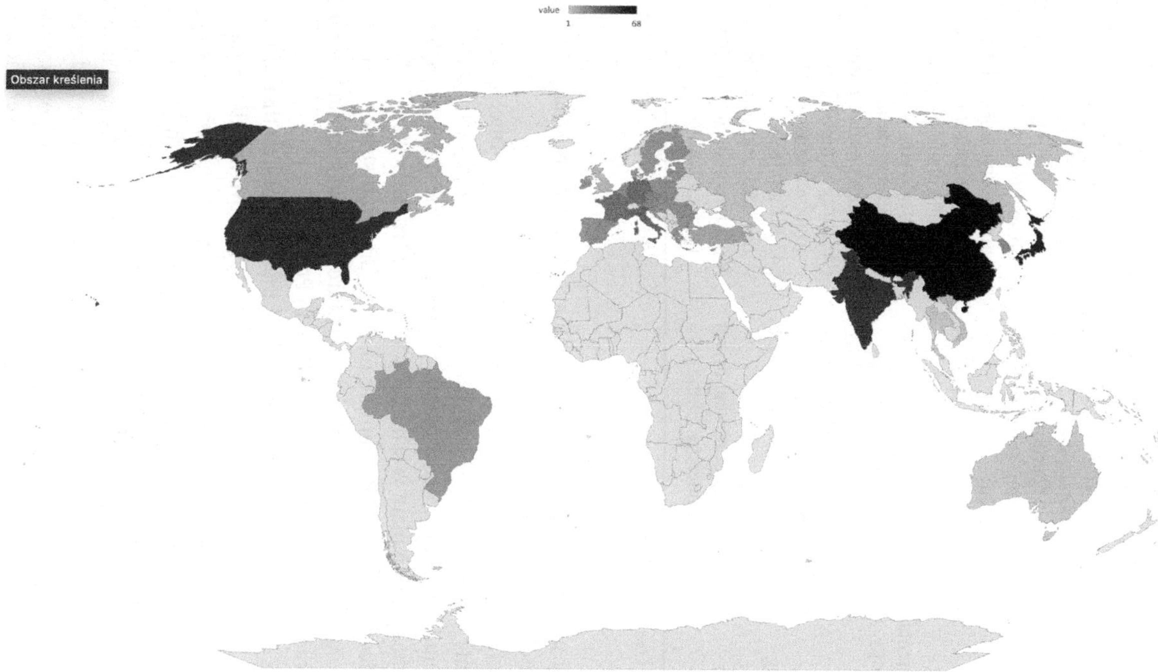

Figure 7.1 Governmental interventions in semiconductors' manufacturing and related activities.

Source: Own elaboration based on Global Trade Alert (2025).

Table 7.1 The U.S. vs European Chips Act

Feature	*U.S. Chips Act*	*European Chips Act*
Aim	Securing national security through reducing dependence on East Asia (particularly China, Taiwan, and South Korea)	Building capacity for cutting-edge chip manufacturing and supporting innovation in specialized areas like automotive and industrial semiconductors
Focus	Manufacturing	All value chain activities
Implementation strategy	Time pressure Centrally administered Seen as national security project, restricted foreign capital involvement	Decentralized implementation Triple helix collaboration Encouraged non-EU capital involvements
Funding	\$52.7 billion + tax credits	€43 billion (mix of EU, national, and private)
Motive	Strong geopolitical driver (countering China)	Moderate geopolitical driver (strategic autonomy)

Source: Own elaboration.

quality and high volume of semiconductors (Bown & Wang, 2024; Duchâtel, 2022).

In effect, some new investments started, including Intel's attempt to create resilient end-to-end value chain in Europe with facilities in Ireland, Germany, and Poland. However, as the investment takes time, the German plant is scheduled to be opened earliest in 2027. The Intel decision is a good example of regionalization strategy, since it envisions manufacturing to take place in Ireland and Germany, whilst assembly and testing facility would be in Poland.

The CRM Act is another example of the EU's policy that directly and indirectly supports reshoring activities. CRM are those naturally occurring resources that are categorized as crucial ones for economic activity and technological development but at the same time are prone to suffer supply disruption risk (including geopolitical risk). These materials often have few or even no substitutes. The Act itself is intended to ensure EU's sustainable access to those materials, which in practice means both diversification of the import sources and boosting domestic production capabilities. The diversification element is meant as part of the de-risking strategy, as the EU's demand for CRM is expected to increase multifold in the forthcoming years (Critical Raw Materials Act, 2024). The CRM Act however includes also stipulations on increasing by 2030 the domestic production capacity of strategic raw materials (Critical Raw Materials Act, 2024):

- EU should be able to extract materials for the production of at least 10% of the EU's consumption of strategic raw materials from its own geological resources,
- EU should be able to process at least 40% of its annual consumption of strategic raw materials,
- EU should be able to produce at least 25% of the EU's annual consumption of strategic raw materials through recycling.

EU is also actively working on standardizing policy that would include standards for CRMs. Adopting technical standardization and consequently harmonizing standards across Member States would result in fewer trade barriers. It will also enable to select policy priorities, like standards to support the recycling of CRMs (Righetti et al., 2025). The strengthening of the value chain is perceived for all stages of the value chain of strategic raw materials. Although the terms "reshoring" or "backshoring" are never explicitly used within the CRM Act, the assumptions of the policy are to boost CRM-related investment in the Europe. Therefore, in a way, we can expect a redirection of capital flows back to the European region.

European reshoring framework or single country approach?

The COVID-19 pandemic outbreak has pushed policy makers to reconsider "a renewed primacy of politics over economics" (De Meyer, 2020). This shift led to the swift and widespread implementation of new reshoring initiatives. The literature reveals examples of developed countries that used financial incentives, infrastructure investments, foreign trade policies and other administrative tools to encourage reshoring, yet a significant number of those was developed mid- and post-pandemic (Table 7.2).

As illustrated in Table 7.2, the potential scope of incentives is significantly broader than those applied by most European countries. Policy makers in EU rarely invest in initiatives that would allow re-skilling and up-skilling human capital to meet the demand of the reshoring companies. Instead, they focus on developing and

Table 7.2 Summary of reshoring initiatives in Europe – chosen countries (2020 onward)

Country		*France*	*UK*	*Germany*	*Poland*
Cost and financial incentives	Financial aids	+			
	Fiscal incentives (e.g. tax reductions and exemptions)	+			+
	Subsidies for reshoring costs	+			
Supply chain	Support for suppliers' research		+		
	Development for suppliers' capabilities (especially SMEs)		+	+	+
	Environmental and human rights regulations for SC			+	
Public administration	Single contact person	+	+		
	Reduction of bureaucracy	+			
Infrastructure	Development of production infrastructure (e.g. industrial areas, scientific parks)				
	Grants for private infrastructure development			+	
	Other infrastructure (e.g. railways, motorways)				+
	Information on availability of plants	+			
	Plant utilities continuity				
Innovation	Innovation policy (e.g. increased collaboration in triple helix, support service for innovation technology)		+	+	
	R&D tax reduction			+	

Table 7.2 (Continued)

Country		*France*	*UK*	*Germany*	*Poland*
Human capital	Human capital development				
	Human capital availability				
Home-country image	Home-country "made in" brand			+	
Protectionism	Duties and tariffs on imports				

Note: The table indicates a "+" only if the implemented frameworks and initiatives have significantly altered the criteria's outlook in the country.

Source: Own elaboration based on Bornert and Musolino (2024) and Elia et al. (2021).

implementing Industry 4.0 solutions that are expected to eventually decrease labour costs through digital transformation. Similarly, compared to other countries – especially the U.S. – they do not protect the market through increased trade barriers which reflects its commitment to keeping the single market open and competitive. The "old" EU member states have taken more proactive steps to promote reshoring, some of them directly translating into financial benefits for companies and some through imposing challenges if they kept their operations offshored. The Eastern Europe countries have however taken on a passive approach. As mentioned in Chapter 2 Poland is seen as one of the most attractive locations for relocating production, yet it lacks any specific regulations addressing reshoring or nearshoring. While Poland provides general incentives for any company bringing industrial production to the country and offers funds for developing SMEs, these solutions are not targeted at specific industries crucial to the economy. This situation is however not very different from the global outlook. The COVID-19 pandemic prompted some other countries, e.g. Japan, India, or Republic of Korea, to introduce reshoring initiatives when they lacked such solutions earlier. The scope of tools was similar, including mostly financial reliefs, infrastructure, and human capital investments (Chang-Gyun, 2020).

Simultaneously to motivating companies to invest in certain countries, trade and industry policies were enacted to reduce engagement with specific geographic regions. A closer examination of Poland's trade and industry policy reveals that it implemented 151 interventions in 2023 and 136 in 2024 (Global Trade Alert, 2025). This is also true for other V4 countries, especially Slovakia and Czechia (Figure 7.2).

In principle, the implemented initiatives are part of a wider discussion on whether the adoption of industrial policies may lead to transforming the GVCs into regional value chains (RVCs) or domestic value chains (DVCs). Literature lacks unambiguous definition of a

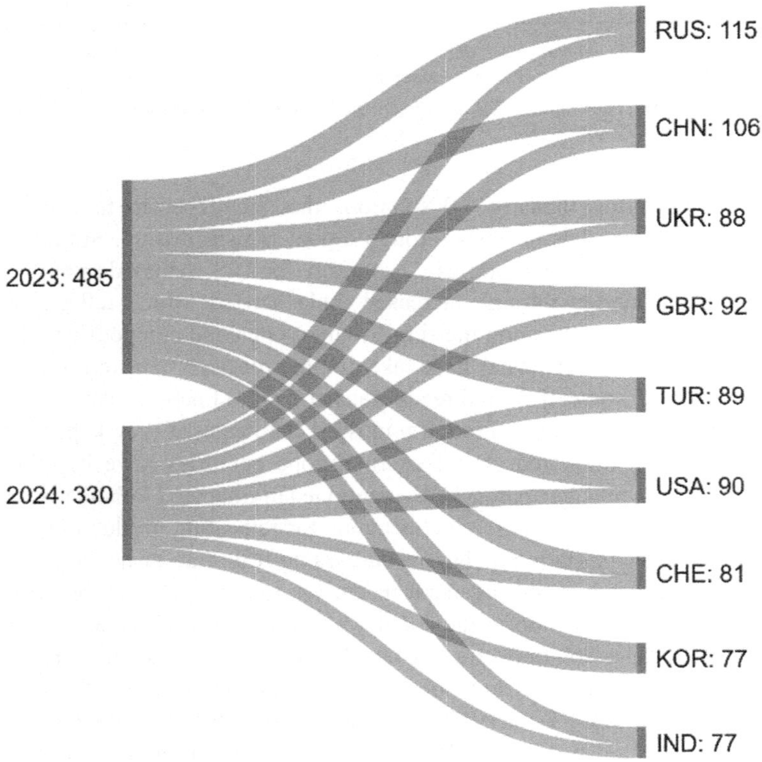

Figure 7.2 Number of V4 interventions (trade and industry policy tools) per chosen affected jurisdiction and year.

Source: Own elaboration based on Global Trade Alert (2025).

Note: Please note that the values for 2023 and 2024 do not reflect the total number of interventions of V4 countries (which amounted in 2023 to: 216 and in 2024 to: 161); certain interventions affected more than single country which is reflected by the chart.

regional value chain but in case of Europe, the RVCs (otherwise European value chains) relate to either "value-chain trade only among EU Member States" producers' (Zachariadis, 2019, p. 4) or to a "situation where two or more EU Member States are jointly involved in producing for some other country or for themselves" (Stöllinger et al., 2018, p. 9). The DVC is referred to when the production stages take place domestically (Elia et al., 2021). It is estimated that between 2000 and 2014 the split between RVC and GVC trade in EU was even, but with modest shifts towards GVC in the following years. Up till the COVID-19 outbreak, the "Factory Europe" was in fact the largest one if compared to "Factory Asia" (Japan, Korea, China, Indonesia, and Taiwan) and "Factory North America" (U.S., Canada, and Mexico). The status quo was attributed to high degree of economic and institutional integration reached by the region. The geographical proximity, no tariff barriers, and relatively low regulatory cross-country challenges facilitated the evolution of "Factory Europe" (Stöllinger et al., 2018). The debate on whether RVCs would – long-term benefit the EU is set against the backdrop of a sustainability and trade openness trade-off (Table 7.3).

Endorsing the development of RVCs in the EU would trigger a series of sustainability-related and trade-related actions. It is

Table 7.3 Impact of RVCs on the sustainability and trade openness

		Trade openness	
		Weakening	*Strengthening*
Sustainability	Weakening	– weakening of international institutions and agreements – return of protectionism – increased interventionism in national policies	
	Strengthening	– increase in greening policies and practices – increase in policies addressing social inequalities – increase in market-driven changes in product and processes	

Source: Own elaboration based on Elia et al. (2021) and Enderwick and Buckley (2020).

anticipated that the policy and economic governance consequences could lead to increased protections and governance interventions, thereby distorting the previously enjoyed trade openness. RVCs, in principle, oppose strengthening trade openness but can simultaneously act as a double-edged sword for sustainability trends. On one hand, European standards in both environmental and human rights areas should drive progress in greening and digital transformation. On the other hand, however, increased interventionism may suppress these effects.

Towards EU's open strategic autonomy?

In 2013 the European Council announced its intention to enhance Europe's defence, technological and industrial capabilities starting the debate on a political concept now known as Open Strategic Autonomy (OSA). OSA is supposed to reflect the EU's "capacity to act autonomously when and where necessary with partners wherever possible" (*Conclusions*, 2013, p. 2). The 2013–2024 timeline marked consecutive periods when the strategic autonomy was defined differently. From 2013 to 2016 it focused mostly on the security and defence issues. Although attempts were made to secure EU's common defence policy, the concept was never fully embraced by various Member States. Between 2017 and 2019, OSA was discussed as a means to secure European interests in light of hostile geopolitical contingencies, including Brexit, the Trump Presidency, and deterioration of U.S.–China relationship. With COVID-19 spread, the focus shifted toward creating resilient supply chains and mitigating trade dependencies. Since 2021 and the following Russian invasion of Ukraine in 2022, the OSA has become a wide concept that covers virtually all EU policy agendas (Damen, 2022).

The OSA is ultimately envisioned as a mitigation to systemic threats which remain problematic to model and predict due to so called "nested interaction effects" (European Parliament. Directorate General for External Policies of the Union., 2021). Nested interaction effects refer to the cascading impact of a series of relatively isolated failures, which can ultimately result in a significant regional (or even global) collapse. Considering the complex interdependencies between sub-systems, policies should focus on creating resilient system able to absorb the shocks. The term resilience originates from Latin (*resilire*) and is understood as "to rebound". The notion has been used across various disciplines but can be traced back to Holling who in 1973 used it to describe the features of a resilient ecosystem. For many scholars resilience is equated to internal, individual traits unrelated to external environment (De Moura & Amelia Tomei, 2021; Waller, 2001). In economics and management resilience is defined as "capability to survive, adapt and grow in a dynamic and uncertain environment" (Rai et al., 2021, p. 12010). The concept is often used interchangeably with the term "robustness" which has a similar yet not identical meaning. Resilience is seen as an ability to return to the initial state whilst robustness means the ability to maintain continuity despite the disruption (Brandon-Jones et al., 2014). While some strategies can boost both resilience and robustness, the key distinction is that resilient systems typically focus on risk mitigation without heavily investing in anticipating and avoiding all types of disruptions. Instead, these firms aim to endure disruptions and concentrate on minimizing their impacts. During COVID-19 pandemic robustness strategies involved multi-sourcing and, in case of multinational enterprises (MNEs), networked multiple location sites. Resilient strategies focused on information sharing procedures and control protocols that would allow systems to re-establish their pre-disruption operations. There is insufficient empirical evidence to claim superiority of either approach, however some research (Jain et al., 2022) suggests resilience-based systems ensure more rapid recovery. Given these experiences, the OSA is expected to provide a resilient-based systematic approach to weather the inherently unpredictable future disruptions.

While the OSA encompasses a broad spectrum of policy areas, this discussion focuses specifically on GVCs and their rewiring. The liberal trade economists advocate that relocation, including reshoring, nearshoring, and friendshoring is not an answer to create resilient GVCs. Gereffi (2020) asserts that robustness strategies, which allow companies to maintain economies of scale and cost efficiency, are more effective, as evidenced by the COVID-19 pandemic. He also emphasizes that in the event of geographical reshuffling, multi-location production sites should be considered over regionalization of production. Relocation will not safeguard the production from certain global disruptions as they would still require import of key materials. That paradoxically may lead to increased GVC insecurity. While these assumptions are theoretically sound, they overlook political agendas that prioritize national security over trade openness. The COVID-19 pandemic demonstrated that, contrary to WTO regulations, trade restrictions were imposed, affecting certain volatile industries (Curran et al., 2021; Curran & Joltreau, 2024). The liberal arguments also do not sufficiently consider deliberate geopolitical power struggle that becomes increasingly visible in recent years. Russian invasion of Ukraine, China–Taiwan tensions, Middle East tensions or even more local contingencies, like coup in Niger have had direct and significant impact on global trade routes, particularly those involving maritime lanes and energy shipping.

Yet, the sluggish economic recovery from the Global Financial Crisis (GFC) of 2009, rising international competition (notably from China and other mid-sized powers), growing social and economic inequalities, and the need for substantial infrastructure investments to support twin transitions, make the economists reconsider the meaning of industrial policies (Aiginger & Ketels, 2024; Mariotti, 2024a). Industrial policies can be viewed as means to achieve technological sovereignty and counter "geo-dirigisme[1]" where necessary capabilities could not be gained by the free market's "invisible hand".

Additionally, in relocation discussion, the trade-off is not only between economic efficiency and geopolitical security but also with the green transition, so intensively debated in EU. Often, the emerging economies do not advocate for high environmental standards, resulting in sizable environmental externalities of production (Crowe & Rawdanowicz, 2023). GVC reconfiguration through relocation will impact domestic and imported character of the carbon emissions (Cadarso et al., 2024). The study by Cadarso et al. (2024) revealed that the EU's imported carbon footprint had several significant hotspots, namely energy-related and transport-related sectors, as well as certain manufacturing industries, e.g. chemical products. The authors develop "climate-reshoring risk combined index", a measure of the change in carbon footprint of EU sectors in reference to reshoring. The reshoring of the production of five strategic for EU products (iron and steel, electrical motors and batteries, chips and circuits, antibiotics, and vaccines) would likely result in the net emissions' reductions. The estimated carbon footprint reduction for iron and steel should amount to 13 MtCO2, for electric motors and batteries to 4 MtCO2 and for antibiotics and vaccines to less than 1 MtCO2. The reshoring would result in a very low increase in domestic emissions for the entire EU and each member state. However, Eastern EU countries are expected to exhibit the highest relative increases. Their findings highlight that relocation could be vital for the OSA, as EU members would be reducing both direct and indirect emissions within their GVCs. The scenario analysis suggests that the effectiveness of achieving low-carbon supply chains through reshoring or nearshoring varies depending on the industry in question. Long-term, the reshoring of production will result in job loss in the offshored countries which could exert pressure on offshore governments and prompt them to upgrade their environmental policies.

The OSA opens not only the debate for GVC reconfiguration through the relocation process but also through investment screening (Tinti, 2025). China has quickly become one of the largest outward investors globally. The investments made by the Chinese capital in Europe are especially prominent in high-tech industries. The EU has launched mandatory information-sharing mechanism to track the flows of foreign direct investments (FDIs) (European Parliament. Directorate General for External Policies of the Union., 2021). In 2008, only eight countries – Denmark, Finland, France, Germany, the Netherlands, Poland, Spain, and the UK – maintained such mechanisms. By 2023, almost all EU states had introduced or strengthened FDI screening procedures, reflecting heightened concerns over national security, technological sovereignty, and economic resilience (Bauerle Danzman & Meunier, 2023). Scholars argue that these mechanisms are shaped not merely by sectoral strategic considerations but by broader efforts to safeguard long-term competitiveness and innovation within distinct national economic models. Historically, Germany and the UK favoured open-market approaches, while France and Italy adhered to state-driven regulatory traditions; however, all have converged toward stricter controls in response to geopolitical pressures. Yet, the existing regulations are limited to coordination of screening the investments without any actual authority to block acquisitions. At the supranational level, the European Commission has sought to harmonize national practices through Regulation No. 452/2019, which established an EU framework for FDI screening (Brugnatelli, 2025). This regulation introduced evaluation criteria focusing on critical infrastructure, advanced technologies, essential services, and sensitive information, alongside recommendations for strategic technology controls. Although the framework does not grant the Commission authority to block investments, it promotes information exchange and advisory cooperation among member states, signalling the EU's ambition to act as a unified political actor. This development aligns with the broader securitization of EU trade and investment policies, positioning the Union as a strategic intermediary amid U.S.–China competition (Meunier & Nicolaidis, 2019). Nonetheless, critics contend that national interests continue to dominate, limiting the EU's capacity to achieve genuine strategic autonomy (Jacobs, 2019). Individual Member States like Germany and France have taken their own actions to impose regulatory restrictions on FDI in critical industries.

In principle, the debate on OSA is gaining momentum. From GVC-perspective it requires to address certain choices on how "open" the strategic autonomy is supposed to be. Mariotti (2024a) points to three overlapping perspectives on OSA:

- the notion that, long-term, openness and strategic autonomy are mutually supportive to achieve fundamental restructuring and transformation of European industry landscape under the current megatrends (Della Posta, 2023; Miró, 2023),
- the notion that steering away from traditional European multilateralism towards political realism could risk the EU falling into the "autonomy trap"; quest for decoupling to achieve self-sufficiency may cost EU its competitive position leading to isolation (Olsthoorn, 2024),
- the notion that in fact openness and autonomy are mutually exclusive and would eventually lead to "decoupling à la carte" where member states' individual pragmatism would prevail (Broeders et al., 2023).

Against the backdrop of increasing geopolitical disruptions, the EU needs to consider long-term impact of the openness and trade dependencies on the resilience capabilities of the EU. The main concern however is that these decisions can no longer be merely "contemplated" but need to be enforced as EU is already losing ground to China and the U.S.

Note

1 Geo-dirigisme means "the idea that markets, if left to their own devices, will underprovide the technological competencies and economic competitiveness necessary to survive and thrive in (…) 'geotech world' (…) a world where technology and geopolitics are increasingly intertwined" (Seidl & Schmitz, 2024, p. 2148–2149).

8 Closing the loop

GVCs and contemporary extensions of Rodrik's dilemma

Rodrik's (2011) globalization trilemma has long served as one of the most influential frameworks for understanding the tension between international economic integration and domestic political structures. Rodrik argued that countries cannot simultaneously pursue deep economic globalization, nation-state sovereignty, and democratic politics. A political economy could sustain any two of these pillars, but not all three. For instance, hyper-globalization combined with democratic accountability necessarily weakens national sovereignty, because global rules require domestic policy convergence. Conversely, sovereignty and democracy limit the scope of globalization, as domestic constituencies impose constraints on the openness of markets. Rodrik's formulation captured a late-20th-century world characterized by relatively stable geopolitical conditions, the expansion of multilateral institutions, and a strong belief in the efficiency of globally dispersed production networks.

The decades following the original trilemma, however, have witnessed profound changes in the global economy that have rendered Rodrik's assumptions increasingly unstable. Between the early 2000s and the 2020s, three structural developments challenged the feasibility of sustaining deep economic integration: the return of great-power rivalry, the weaponization of interdependence, and the rise of national security logics within economic policy. As global value chains (GVCs) deepened – particularly through the rapid expansion of China as the "world's factory" – countries also became increasingly exposed to geopolitical vulnerabilities embedded within those very networks. Events such as the U.S.–China trade war, Russia's invasion in Ukraine and subsequent sanctions, the COVID-19 pandemic, semiconductor

DOI: 10.4324/9781003724803-8

export controls, and disruptions to critical infrastructure revealed the fragility of a system built on the assumption that states would continue to treat economic interdependence as an unqualified good.

This new environment has foregrounded security – an element largely implicit or backgrounded in Rodrik's original trilemma. The post-Cold War moment, in which Rodrik theorized, assumed a relatively benign security environment in which states did not actively weaponize GVCs or technological dependency. Today, however, the pursuit of national security has become a dominant driver of economic policy. States increasingly evaluate global production networks not only in terms of cost and efficiency, but also in terms of exposure to rival powers, control over critical technologies, and resilience to politically motivated disruptions. This shift has produced widespread policy initiatives promoting reshoring, nearshoring, friendshoring, and industrial decoupling – developments that the original globalization trilemma cannot fully explain.

To capture these contemporary dynamics, a revised theoretical lens is necessary. This research advances the "Globalization-Sovereignty-Resilience Trilemma", which posits that no state can simultaneously maximize:

- deep globalization,
- full sovereignty,
- resilience against geopolitical adversaries.

Deep globalization entails integration through GVCs; sovereignty reflects unilateral control over industrial policy, technology standards, and strategic sectors; and resilience refers to safeguarding against adversarial leverage and the capacity to protect national interests in crises. The three cannot coexist in their fullest form. Pursuing globalization and sovereignty without resilience – as in the pre-2020 global economy – exposes states to strategic vulnerabilities. Maximizing sovereignty and resilience, which is reflected in contemporary reshoring and industrial policy, necessarily curtails the depth of global integration. Conversely, maintaining globalization and resilience requires compromises in sovereign policy autonomy, such as reliance on harmonized standards or collective security arrangements that limit domestic discretion.

This reconfigured trilemma does not replace Rodrik's (2011) but rather updates it for an era in which security has become central to economic governance. It provides a macro-level framework that explains why states and firms are now reorganizing production networks around geopolitical blocs and why efficiency considerations no longer dominate global strategy. Crucially, this trilemma enables a new theoretical extension to Transaction Cost Economics (TCE). Classic TCE explains firm governance choices, such as outsourcing or offshoring, based on the minimization of transaction hazards related to uncertainty, asset specificity, and frequency. Yet TCE was developed for market-driven environments in which hazards were primarily behavioural and contractual. Today's geopolitical environment introduces non-market transaction hazards that TCE does not explicitly theorize: sovereign opportunism, state-imposed switching costs, regulatory discontinuities triggered by sanctions, and politically motivated disruptions to supply routes. These hazards originate not in market dynamics but in strategic interactions between states.

Both the empirical research in Chapters 4 and 5, and the case study from Chapter 6 enable us to translate this dilemma to the firm-level considerations. By embedding the "Globalization-Sovereignty-Resilience Trilemma" into TCE, one can propose a systematic extension: transaction hazards increasingly emerge from geopolitical location risks, not simply from partner behaviour. This contributes to TCE by introducing a new category of hazard – sovereign opportunism risk – and by expanding uncertainty to include geopolitical uncertainty, which is unpredictable, exogenous, and non-contractible. Under these conditions, offshoring becomes costlier not because suppliers act opportunistically but because states do. Reshoring thus becomes a form of (geo)political internalization, reducing exposure to external sovereign risk. TCE thereby evolves from a theory of market frictions to a theory encompassing geopolitical-security transaction costs.

Therefore, the macro-level trilemma can have an important micro-level analogue: the "Firm-level Globalization Trilemma", which explains why companies increasingly pursue reshoring despite significant cost disadvantages. Like states, firms cannot simultaneously maintain:

- global efficiency optimization,
- strategic autonomy in operations,
- resilience.

Again, a firm can combine efficiency and resilience, but doing so sacrifices autonomy because offshoring and global partnerships

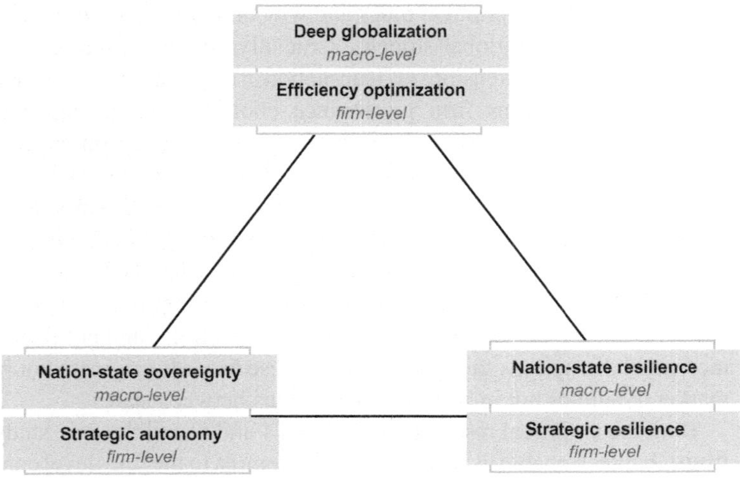

Figure 8.1 Contemporary extensions of Rodrik's dilemma.
Source: Own elaboration.

inherently create dependence on foreign jurisdictions, standards, and the willingness of others to trade. Conversely, a firm may achieve efficiency and autonomy through global sourcing, yet this configuration leaves it exposed to geopolitical risk, as supply chains remain vulnerable to sanctions, export controls, or political disruptions. Finally, prioritizing autonomy and resilience – for example, by reshoring production and investing in proprietary technology – enhances independence and self-reliance but comes at the cost of efficiency optimization, as firms forgo the benefits of global scale and low-cost sourcing in favour of strategic security (Figure 8.1).

Future of the GVC reconfiguration?

The last decade has triggered profound shift in how we perceive the world after decades of globalization. In the proposed changes to Rodrik's trilemma, we still emphasize deep globalization and its benefits for companies. At the same time, however, we observe an increasingly pronounced discussion on its reversal and the rewiring of GVCs. Scholars refer to "deglobalization" as a retreat from global integration, giving way to "regionalization" or "islandization" characterized by relocation strategies, either reshoring or nearshoring within politically friendly regions (Enderwick & Buckley, 2020; Witt et al., 2023). Some use the term "slowbalization" which suggests a gradual slowdown in globalization, though it fails to capture the instability and fluctuating nature of foreign direct investment (FDI). Some scholars propose that globalization is increasingly vulnerable to geopolitical pressures, predicting once again the dominance of geopolitics over geoeconomics (Mariotti, 2024a). They argue that neither globalization nor deglobalization will dominate, but instead, an ongoing, unstable interplay between the two forces will continue (Cui et al., 2023; Mariotti, 2024b). Mariotti (2024b, p. 5) coins the term "win-lose globalization" which aims to reflect the current state of "growing disparity between the losers and winners of the globalization".

Regardless of the nomenclature used, the common sentiment prevails that the liberal international economic order – that once underpinned globalization – is currently undergoing a significant transformation. Luo (2024) introduces the concept of "fragmented globalization", a term that captures the retreat from multilateralism and the rise of nationalistic interventionism. This new paradigm does not entail a complete reversal of globalization but its reconfiguration where national interest takes precedence. This shift has major implications, especially for international business and GVC-related research.

Nationalistic interventionism can be understood as states' intervention in international affairs aimed at protecting and promoting domestic interests (Luo, 2024; Van Assche, 2025). Its rise can be attributed to the growing scepticism about the efficacy of global institutions. It is constantly challenged with the supply chain resilience, techno-nationalism and more and more visible sustainability drive. Yet, scholars claim that fragmented globalization also means selective economic integration based on geopolitical alignments. While countries may decouple in strategic sectors (e.g. semiconductors), they will likely continue to cooperate on global issues like climate change. This dual approach is known as "pragmatic inclusivity", which acknowledges that states may simultaneously engage in both rivalry and collaboration (Hoekman, 2024). A good example can be the current a tentative agreement reached between the U.S. and China on the supply of rare earth elements. China has allegedly agreed to provide American firms with rare earth metals and magnets in exchange for easing visa restrictions for Chinese students. The agreement reflects a broader effort by both nations to stabilize trade relations and reduce geopolitical tensions, depicting the pragmatic inclusivity phenomenon. In effect, what we can expect, especially in terms of GVC reconfiguration, is finding a middle ground between the extremes of globalization and deglobalization. This may mean regionalization, political conditionality, and strategic autonomy as the guiding logics of international trade and investment engagement.

The GVC reconfiguration can take on various approaches which include both alterations of governance modes and geographical relocation. This phenomenon is known as springboard rerouting (Luo & Witt, 2022). Although the current geopolitical developments imply general decline of international cooperation and interdependence, the decoupling is expected among the key players like China, the U.S. and their allies (Ando et al., 2024). Meanwhile this shift also implies the rise of other, previously non-existent or underappreciated trade and investment ties, now especially benefiting some emerging markets. Current economic trends also suggest that risks once viewed as country-specific are now increasingly seen as regional in nature, thereby influencing the GVCs' reconfiguration. Faber et al. (2025) indicate that the openness of the global economy is stagnating which is evidenced by the macroeconomic data. The world today is no longer matching the pre-GFC crisis era, and the recent years of geopolitical tensions have only accelerated the shift in trends. It is still debateable whether reshoring is as dominant as had been expected but the ratio of value added to gross output in the manufacturing sector has been indicating a trend toward GVC shortening – and thus reshoring – since as early as 2014.

Yet, decoupling and the related to this relocation strategies are also dependent on the industries and goods we consider. Jiang and Xing (2025) claim that the sectors primarily engaged in raw material trade exhibit larger disparities between forward and backward GVC integration than sectors centred on intermediate goods. Likewise, discrepancies appear when we consider country profile; countries with well-developed, large-scale economies, complete manufacturing chains, and robust domestic consumption demonstrate stronger global economic integration. Additionally, these countries are more capable of withstanding external shocks and global market fluctuations. Having said that, the current geopolitical and economic developments have impacted the country's embeddedness in GVCs to various degree. Notably, China's backward GVC decoupling level has remained relatively stable compared to its forward decoupling degree. This can be attributed to China's expansive domestic market and its highly autonomous and integrated supply chain network. Simultaneously, China entered into multilateral trade agreements to mitigate the effects of direct U.S. trade restrictions. In the short term, transshipment export strategies have also proven effective in circumventing such barriers, thereby sustaining China's export performance. Conteduca et al. (2025) stress that the U.S. has pursued a decoupling strategy from China already since 2018, while the EU's direct dependence on Chinese imports only began to decline markedly in 2023. This decoupling has been most evident in advanced technology products and paradoxically, for critical goods (e.g. related to the energy transition), the share of imports from China has increased. The scholars predict that this trade reconfiguration seems to be a long-term and deliberate one, rather than a temporary adjustment.

At the backdrop of these considerations, this monograph showcases how the contemporary megatrends such as sustainability drive, advanced digitalization, and unpredictable geopolitical disruptions are reshaping international production and investment patterns. While acknowledging the importance of all three, the core analytical focus is placed on geopolitics since this megatrend is said to impact especially CEE countries and their internationalization strategies. Contrary to widespread expectations relocation pathway is not the most commonly adaptive response of multinational enterprises (MNEs) that emerges following the COVID-19 pandemic, sanctions, and increasing uncertainty. Yet it is significant enough to deserve specific attention to understand its underlying mechanism and drivers. The study's value-added lies in the development of a conceptual model that distinguishes between the drivers of relocation under geopolitical disruption and those associated with more conventional motives, such as market- and cost-orientation. It identifies a set of geopolitical antecedents – including cyberattacks in the host country, the formation of geopolitical blocs, the imposition of trade sanctions, transformations in transport organization, and relocation-supportive policies – that exert a systemic influence over more traditional economic factors, such as wage differentials or investment incentives. It is crucial to understand that these results are embedding relocation in the geopolitical contingency only and show how these antecedents act as catalysts for reshoring in such geopolitically-disturbed ecosystem.

The study aims at providing a more nuanced understanding of geopolitically-driven relocation behaviour than the existing literature offers. The discussion however is moved beyond theoretical development by applying the developed model to a case study, illustrating the explanatory potential of its framework with use of a real-life example. The results are also relevant for the policy-level discussion, evaluating whether the research findings align with the current orientation of the OSA framework of the European Union (EU) or at least the industrial strategies of individual EU members. By doing so, it provides a bridge between academic insights and practical policy considerations, offering direction for both future research and decision-making. The monograph's approach highlighting interconnectedness among geopolitical and economic factors not only provides a new lens through which to interpret relocation mechanism but also opens new research areas for investigating how firms and states might strategically respond to the evolving global order.

For decades research on GVCs, including offshoring and reshoring investigations, were assuming an implicit belief of the stability of the international order. The era of globalization which was marked by deepening interdependence, widespread of free trade agreements, and the relative absence of large-scale geopolitical tensions (at least among the key global trade partners) fostered the notion that all and every country was striving for achieving shared goal of prosperity. However, this belief seems to have proven misplaced. The re-emergence of geopolitical rivalries, trade tensions leading to open trade wars, introduction of sanctions, decoupling, and other developments have dismantled these long-standing assumptions. Now, scholars including Antràs (2020), Gereffi (Gereffi, Lim, et al., 2021; Gereffi, Posthuma, et al., 2021) or Baldwin and Freeman (2022) argue that GVC studies need to be reoriented to account for geopolitics. There is a common consensus that companies have shifted from searching for optimal outcomes based on comparative advantage to choosing second-best solutions mitigating potential risks. Recent developments, such as U.S.–China decoupling, the EU's push for strategic autonomy, military deployments and even the supply chain bottlenecks during COVID-19, only underscore the urgency of this shift. Geopolitics seems to increasingly determine investment decisions, sourcing strategies, and trade flows. Yet, the existing literature remains overly focused on traditional understanding of performance neglecting a broader systemic overview of risks. As the international environment becomes more volatile and uncertain, it is essential for GVC research to incorporate geopolitical analysis, not only to better understand current trends but also to support policymakers and firms in navigating a world where the pursuit of stability is no longer guaranteed.

The monograph inevitably has its limitations, as it can address only a certain scope of issues. Given the rapid pace of change and the continual emergence of new geopolitical dynamics, further studies on intersection between geopolitics and international business are needed. For instance, recent global survey of supply-chain executives has shown that a vast majority of companies is reassessing their strategies and investments in anticipation of Trump's new regulations. These adjustments align with the three pathways identified in Chapter 4 of this volume and are supposed to mitigate the costs that the everchanging tariffs have offset. Moreover, the reshoring, nearshoring, and friendshoring strategies are likely to become more applied since politically neutral hotspots are seen as affordable alternatives offering insulation from global political instability. However, new challenges emerge, for example the lack of regulatory harmonization with these countries that brings forth serious scalability issues. Moreover, these strategies, especially friendshoring, can also backfire. A recent intervention of a U.S.–Japan takeover in steel and aluminium industry has shown even between close allies, unpredictable protectionism can occur. Determining who qualifies as and remains a long-term ally is increasingly difficult, making supply chain planning more complex.

Yet, despite the push to reshore the production, companies continue to value global integration. The strategies still most evoked by executives remains the diversification trajectory. The supply chains are expected to regionalize, to reduce transportation costs and mitigate operational risk related to ongoing armed conflicts. Ultimately, businesses are seeking a balance between resilience and efficiency in an increasingly volatile global trade environment. This aim brings forward two major considerations that are likely to shape the future of GVCs. First, the intersection of geopolitics and sustainability will become increasingly significant; particularly as firms seek to comply with evolving regulatory standards imposed by the EU, while simultaneously navigating geopolitical risks. This dual pressure is expected to influence the restructuring of GVCs to a significant degree. Second, the role of digital transformation, including automation and robotics, warrants attention (Calatayud & Rochina-Barrachina, 2025; Dachs & Wolfmayr, 2025). Theoretically, digital developments were expected to have accelerated relocation strategies, but the current empirical evidence does not fully support this claim. However, such effects may become more pronounced in an era of heightened geopolitical disruption requiring further investigation.

References

Abadie, A., & Gardeazabal, J. (2003). The Economic Costs of Conflict: A Case Study of the Basque Country. *American Economic Review*, 93(1), 113–132. https://doi.org/10.1257/000282803321455188

Abadie, A., & Gardeazabal, J. (2008). Terrorism and the World Economy. *European Economic Review*, 52(1), 1–27. https://doi.org/10.1016/j.euroecorev.2007.08.005

Aggarwal, V., & Urata, S. (2006). *Bilateral Trade Agreements in the Asia-Pacific Origins, Evolution, and Implications*. Routledge.

Ahir, H., Bloom, N., & Furceri, D. (2019). New Index Tracks Trade Uncertainty across the Globe. *International Monetary Fund; IMFBlog*. www.imf.org/en/Blogs/Articles/2019/09/09/blog-new-index-tracks-trade-uncertainty-across-the-globe

Aiginger, K., & Ketels, C. (2024). Industrial Policy Reloaded. *Journal of Industry, Competition and Trade*, 24(1), 7, s10842-024-00415–00418. https://doi.org/10.1007/s10842-024-00415-8

Aiyar, S., Malacrino, D., & Presbitero, A. F. (2024). Investing in Friends: The Role of Geopolitical Alignment in FDI Flows. *European Journal of Political Economy*, 83, 102508. https://doi.org/10.1016/j.ejpoleco.2024.102508

Akadiri, S. S., Eluwole, K. K., Akadiri, A. C., & Avci, T. (2020). Does Causality between Geopolitical Risk, Tourism and Economic Growth Matter? Evidence from Turkey. *Journal of Hospitality and Tourism Management*, 43, 273–277. https://doi.org/10.1016/j.jhtm.2019.09.002

Ando, M., Hayakawa, K., & Kimura, F. (2024). Supply Chain Decoupling: Geopolitical Debates and Economic Dynamism in East Asia. *Asian Economic Policy Review*, 19(1), 62–79. https://doi.org/10.1111/aepr.12439

Antras, P. (2003). Firms, Contracts, and Trade Structure. *The Quarterly Journal of Economics*, 118(4), 1375–1418. https://doi.org/10.1162/003355303322552829

Antràs, P. (2020). *De-Globalisation? Global Value Chains in the Post-COVID-19 Age* (No. w28115; p. w28115). National Bureau of Economic Research. https://doi.org/10.3386/w28115

Antràs, P., & Chor, D. (2013). Organizing the Global Value Chain. *Econometrica*, 81(6), 2127–2204. https://doi.org/10.3982/ECTA10813

Arte, P., & Larimo, J. (2019). Taking Stock of Foreign Divestment: Insights and Recommendations from Three Decades of Contemporary Literature. *International Business Review*, 28(6), 101599. https://doi.org/10.1016/j.ibusrev.2019.101599

Ascani, A., Bettarelli, L., Resmini, L., & Balland, P.-A. (2020). Global Networks, Local Specialisation and Regional Patterns of Innovation. *Research Policy*, 49(8), 104031. https://doi.org/10.1016/j.respol.2020.104031

Baldwin, R. (2013). Global Supply Chains: Why They Emerged, Why They Matter, and Where They Are Going. In D. Elms & P. Low (Eds), *Global Value Chains in a Changing World* (pp. 13–59). World Trade Organization.

Baldwin, R. (2016). The World Trade Organization and the Future of Multilateralism. *Journal of Economic Perspectives*, 30(1), 95–116. https://doi.org/10.1257/jep.30.1.95

Baldwin, R., & Freeman, R. (2022). Risks and Global Supply Chains: What We Know and What We Need to Know. *Annual Review of Economics*, 14(1), 153–180. https://doi.org/10.1146/annurev-economics-051420-113737

Bandyopadhyay, S., Sandler, T., & Younas, J. (2014). Foreign Direct Investment, Aid, and Terrorism. *Oxford Economic Papers*, 66(1), 25–50. https://doi.org/10.1093/oep/gpt026

Barbieri, P., Boffelli, A., Elia, S., Fratocchi, L., Kalchschmidt, M., & Samson, D. (2020). What Can We Learn About Reshoring after Covid-19? *Operations Management Research*, 13(3–4), 131–136. https://doi.org/10.1007/s12063-020-00160-1

Barbieri, P., Ciabuschi, F., Fratocchi, L., & Vignoli, M. (2018). What Do We Know About Manufacturing Reshoring? *Journal of Global Operations and Strategic Sourcing*, 11(1), 79–122. https://doi.org/10.1108/JGOSS-02-2017-0004

Bauerle Danzman, S., & Meunier, S. (2023). Naïve No More: Foreign Direct Investment Screening in the European Union. *Global Policy*, 14(S3), 40–53. https://doi.org/10.1111/1758-5899.13215

Becko, J. S. (2024). A Theory of Economic Sanctions as Terms-of-Trade Manipulation. *Journal of International Economics*, 150, 103898. https://doi.org/10.1016/j.jinteco.2024.103898

Bednarski, L., Roscoe, S., Blome, C., & Schleper, M. C. (2023). Geopolitical Disruptions in Global Supply Chains: A State-of-the-Art Literature Review. *Production Planning & Control*, 1–27. https://doi.org/10.1080/09537287.2023.2286283

Bhagwat, J., & Shaparov, A. (2024). The Red Sea Crisis: Need for Alternative International Transport Routes. *Strategic Affairs*, LIX(21), 10–16.

Bhattacharjee, A., Sidana, N., Goel, R., Shukre, A., & Singh, T. (2024). Cross-Border Ripples: Investigating Stock Market Responses to Israel-Hamas Conflict in Trading Partner Nations Using Event Study Method. *Journal of Economic Studies*. https://doi.org/10.1108/JES-05-2024-0291

Bhaumik, S. K., Driffield, N., Estrin, S., & Razeq, Z. M. (2025). Geopolitical Alignment, Outside Options, and Inward FDI: An Integrated Framework and Policy Pathways. *Journal of International Business Policy*. https://doi.org/10.1057/s42214-025-00212-y

Blažek, J., & Lypianin, A. (2024). Geopolitical Decoupling and Global ProductionNetworks: The Case of Ukrainian Industries after the 2014 Crimean Annexation. *Journal of Economic Geography*, 24(1), 23–40. https://doi.org/10.1093/jeg/lbad026

Bornert, X., & Musolino, D. (2024). The Manufacturing Reshoring Phenomenon: A Policy-Oriented Analysis of Factors Driving the Location Decision. *Economies*, 12(5), 100. https://doi.org/10.3390/economies12050100

Bouët, A., Sall, L. M., & Zheng, Y. (2024). *Trump 2.0 Tariffs: What Cost for the World Economy?* CEPII – Policy Brief No 49. www.cepii.fr/PDF_PUB/pb/2024/pb2024-49.pdf

Bown, C. P., & Wang, D. (2024). Semiconductors and Modern Industrial Policy. *Journal of Economic Perspectives*, 38(4), 81–110. https://doi.org/10.1257/jep.38.4.81

Brandon-Jones, E., Squire, B., Autry, C. W., & Petersen, K. J. (2014). A Contingent Resource-Based Perspective of Supply Chain Resilience and Robustness. *Journal of Supply Chain Management*, 50(3), 55–73. https://doi.org/10.1111/jscm.12050

Brennan, L., & Rakhmatullin, R. (2017). Transnationalizing Smart Specialization Strategy. In S. Radosevic, A. Curaj, R.u Gheorghiu, L. Andreescu & I. Wade (Eds), *Advances in the Theory and Practice of Smart Specialization* (pp. 249–268). Elsevier. https://doi.org/10.1016/B978-0-12-804137-6.00011-5

Broeders, D., Cristiano, F., & Kaminska, M. (2023). In Search of Digital Sovereignty and Strategic Autonomy: Normative Power Europe to the Test of Its Geopolitical Ambitions. *JCMS: Journal of Common Market Studies*, 61(5), 1261–1280. https://doi.org/10.1111/jcms.13462

Brugnatelli, N. (2025). The Evolution of Chinese FDI in Europe and Its Implications for Technological Interdependence: A Geoeconomic Perspective. *The International Spectator*, 60(3), 101–116. https://doi.org/10.1080/03932729.2025.2519042

Buckley, P. J. (2011). International Integration and Coordination in the Global Factory. *Management International Review*, 51(2), 269–283. https://doi.org/10.1007/s11575-011-0075-2

Buckley, P. J. (2023). Corporate Reactions to the Fracturing of the Global Economy. *International Business Review*, 32(6), 102014. https://doi.org/10.1016/j.ibusrev.2022.102014

Bunel, B., Van Assche, A., & Aguilar-Delgado, N. (2022). *The WTO under Azevêdo: Between a Rock and a Hard Place*. HEC Montreal Centre for Case Studies.

Burgers, C., Brugman, B. C., & Boeynaems, A. (2019). Systematic Literature Reviews: Four Applications for Interdisciplinary Research. *Journal of Pragmatics*, 145, 102–109. https://doi.org/10.1016/j.pragma.2019.04.004

Cadarso, M.-A., García-Alaminos, Á., López, L., Tobarra, M.-A., Ortiz, M., Curran, L., Joltreau, T., Gnekpe, C., Pedersen, T., Zafrilla, J., Mroczek-Dąbrowska, K., Jankowska, B., Kania, A., Mińska-Struzik, E., Matysek-Jędrych, A., Gomez, N., Monsalve, F., & Arce, G. (2024). *Recent and Emerging Trends of GVCs and MNEs: Impacts on the Environment*. https://twinseeds.eu/wp-content/uploads/2024/10/WP4-Report.pdf

Calatayud, C., & Rochina-Barrachina, M. E. (2025). Robots and Firm Reshoring. *Industry and Innovation*, 1–20. https://doi.org/10.1080/13662716.2025.2495758

Caldara, D., & Iacoviello, M. (2022). Measuring Geopolitical Risk. *American Economic Review*, 112(4), 1194–1225. https://doi.org/10.1257/aer.20191823

Cascio, J. (2020). *Facing the Age of Chaos*. https://medium.com/@cascio/facing-the-age-of-chaos-b00687b1f51d

Casson, M. (2021). International Business Policy in An Age of Political Turbulence. *Journal of World Business*, 56(6), 101263. https://doi.org/10.1016/j.jwb.2021.101263

Cavaciuti-Wishart, E., Heading, S., Kohler, K., & Zahidi, S. (2024). *Global Risks Report 2024*. World Economic Forum. www.weforum.org/publications/global-risks-report-2024/

Chang-Gyun, L. (2020, May 10). Pandemic Prompts Companies to Weigh Reshoring. *Korea Joong Ang Daily*. https://koreajoongangdaily.joins.com/2020/05/10/finance/company-korean-companies-korea-companies/20200510203500109.html

Cipollina, M., & Dal Bianco, S. (2025). Trade Sanctions and Global Value Chains: The Role of Financial Development and Capital Openness in Emerging Markets. *Emerging Markets Review*, 67, 101281. https://doi.org/10.1016/j.ememar.2025.101281

Ciriminna, R., Della Pina, C., Luque, R., & Pagliaro, M. (2024). Reshoring Fine Chemical and Pharmaceutical Productions. *Organic Process Research & Development*, 28(8), 3026–3034. https://doi.org/10.1021/acs.oprd.4c00219

Clausing, K., & Obstfeld, M. (2024). Trump's 2025 Tariff Threats. *Intereconomics*, 59(4), 243–244. https://doi.org/10.2478/ie-2024-0048

Coe, N. M., Dicken, P., & Hess, M. (2008). Global Production Networks: Realizing the Potential. *Journal of Economic Geography*, 8(3), 271–295. https://doi.org/10.1093/jeg/lbn002

Comtrade Database. (2024). *[Data set]*. United Nations. https://comtradeplus.un.org/

Conclusions. (2013). European Council. https://data.consilium.europa.eu/doc/document/ST-217-2013-INIT/en/pdf

Conteduca, F. P., Giglioli, S., Giordano, C., Mancini, M., & Panon, L. (2025). Trade Fragmentation Unveiled: Five Facts on the Reconfiguration of Global, US and EU Trade. *Journal of Industrial and Business Economics*. https://doi.org/10.1007/s40812-024-00337-w

Contractor, F. J. (2025). Assessing the Economic Impact of Tariffs: Adaptations by Multinationals and Traders to Mitigate Tariffs. *Review of International Business and Strategy*, 35(2/3), 190–213. https://doi.org/10.1108/RIBS-01-2025-0013

Critical Raw Materials Act. (2024). European Comission. https://single-market-economy.ec.europa.eu/sectors/raw-materials/areas-specific-interest/critical-raw-materials/critical-raw-materials-act_en#documents

Crowe, D., & Rawdanowicz, Ł. (2023). *Risks and Opportunities of Reshaping Global Value Chains* (OECD Economics Department Working Papers No. 1762; OECD Economics Department Working Papers, Vol. 1762). https://doi.org/10.1787/f758afe8-en

Csurgai, G. (2017). Geoeconomic Strategies and Economic Intelligence. In J. M. Munoz (Ed), *Advances in Geoeconomics* (1st edn). Routledge. https://doi.org/10.4324/9781315312132

Cuervo-Cazurra, A., Doz, Y., & Gaur, A. (2020). Skepticism of Globalization and Global Strategy: Increasing Regulations and Countervailing Strategies. *Global Strategy Journal*, 10(1), 3–31. https://doi.org/10.1002/gsj.1374

Cui, V., Vertinsky, I., Wang, Y., & Zhou, D. (2023). Decoupling in International Business: The 'New' Vulnerability of Globalization and MNEs' Response Strategies. *Journal of International Business Studies*, 54(8), 1562–1576. https://doi.org/10.1057/s41267-023-00602-5

Curran, L., Eckhardt, J., & Lee, J. (2021). The Trade Policy Response to COVID-19 and Its Implications for International Business. *Critical Perspectives on International Business*, 17(2), 252–320. https://doi.org/10.1108/cpoib-05-2020-0041

Curran, L., & Joltreau, T. (2024). *Shifting GVCs and the Pandemic EU Policy Responses to Support Resilience* (Twin Seeds Policy Brief). https://twinseeds.eu/wp-content/uploads/2024/01/TWIN-SEEDS-Policy-brief-1.pdf

D'Ambrosio, A., & Lavoratori, K. (2025). Reshoring to Survive? The Other Side of De-globalization. *Journal of Industrial and Business Economics*. https://doi.org/10.1007/s40812-025-00342-7

Dachs, B., Kinkel, S., & Jäger, A. (2019). Bringing It All Back Home? Backshoring of Manufacturing Activities and the Adoption of Industry 4.0 Technologies. *Journal of World Business*, 54(6), 101017. https://doi.org/10.1016/j.jwb.2019.101017

Dachs, B., & Wolfmayr, A. (2025). Digital Production Technologies and Exports. *Industry and Innovation*, 1–21. https://doi.org/10.1080/13662716.2024.2421952

Damen, M. (2022). *EU Strategic Autonomy 2013-2023. From Concept to Capacity (EU Strategic Autonomy Monitor)*. European Parliamentary Research Service.

De Marchi, V., & Gereffi, G. (2023). Using the Global Value Chain Framework to Analyse and Tackle Global Environmental Crises. *Journal of Industrial and Business Economics,* 50(1), 149–159. https://doi.org/10.1007/s40812-022-00253-x

De Meyer, A. (2020, April 24). It Won't Be Business as Usual after Covid-19. *The Straits Times*. https://ink.library.smu.edu.sg/cgi/viewcontent.cgi?article=7557&context=lkcsb_research

De Moura, D., & Amelia Tomei, P. (2021). Strategic Management of Organizational Resilience (SMOR): A Framework Proposition. *Review of Business Management,* 23(3), 536–556. https://doi.org/10.7819/rbgn.v.23i3.4118

De Souza, G., Hu, N., Li, H., & Mei, Y. (2024). (Trade) War and Peace: How to Impose International Trade Sanctions. *Journal of Monetary Economics,* 146, 103572. https://doi.org/10.1016/j.jmoneco.2024.103572

De Witte, B. (2025). Internal Market Legislation as European Public Policy. *Revista de Derecho Comunitario Europeo*, 80, 11–17. https://doi.org/10.18042/cepc/rdce.80.01

Delis, A., Driffield, N., & Temouri, Y. (2019). The Global Recession and the Shift to Re-shoring: Myth or Reality? *Journal of Business Research*, 103, 632–643. https://doi.org/10.1016/j.jbusres.2017.09.054

Della Posta, P. (2023). The European Union in the Age of Slowbalisation. *Journal of Policy Modeling*, 45(4), 833–847. https://doi.org/10.1016/j.jpolmod.2023.07.006

Dermine, P., & Patrin, M. (2026). Between Law and Politics—The Emergence of an EU Industrial Policy. *Governance*, 39(1), e70085. https://doi.org/10.1111/gove.70085

Di Stefano, C., Fratocchi, L., Martínez-Mora, C., & Merino, F. (2024). Manufacturing Reshoring and Sustainable Development Goals: A Home Versus Host Country Perspective. *Sustainable Development,* 32(1), 863–875. https://doi.org/10.1002/sd.2710

Di Stefano, E., Giovannetti, G., Mancini, M., Marvasi, E., & Vannelli, G. (2022). Reshoring and Plant Closures in Covid-19 Times: Evidence from

Italian MNEs. *International Economics,* 172, 255–277. https://doi.org/10.1016/j.inteco.2022.09.009

Dreher, A. (2006). Does Globalization Affect Growth? Evidence from a New Index of Globalization. *Applied Economics*, 38(10), 1091–1110. https://doi.org/10.1080/00036840500392078

Duchâtel, M. (2022). *Semiconductors in Europe: The Return of Industrial Policy [Policy Brief]*. Institut Montaigne. www.institutmontaigne.org/resources/pdfs/publications/europe-new-geopolitics-technology-1.pdf

Economic and Market Report Global and EU Auto Industry: Full Year 2024. (2025). ACEA. www.acea.auto/files/Economic_and_Market_Report-Full_year_2024.pdf

Elia, S., Fratocchi, L., Barbieri, P., Boffellid, A., & Kalchschmidt, M. (2021). Post-pandemic Reconfiguration from Global to Domestic and Regional Value Chains: The Role of Industrial Policies. *Transnational Corporations Journal*, 28(2), 67–96.

Enderwick, P., & Buckley, P. J. (2020). Rising Regionalization: Will the Post-COVID-19 World See a Retreat from Globalization. *Transnational Corporations*, 27(2), 99–112.

European Parliament. Directorate General for External Policies of the Union. (2021). *Post Covid-19 Value Chains: Options for Reshoring Production Back to Europe in a Globalised Economy.* Publications Office. https://data.europa.eu/doi/10.2861/428

Evenett, S. J. (2022). What Endgame for the Deglobalisation Narrative? *Intereconomics*, 57(6), 345–351. https://doi.org/10.1007/s10272-022-1085-y

Evenett, S. J., & Muendler, M.-A. (2025). *Executing Trump's Campaign Pledges on Tariffs Won't Restore Manufacturing in the Rust Belt—Or Elsewhere for that Matter*. Global Trade Alert. https://ricardo-dashboard.s3.eu-west-1.amazonaws.com/reports/1737367923024_c%20Brief%204.pdf

Evers, N., Ojala, A., Sousa, C. M. P., & Criado-Rialp, A. (2023). Unraveling Business Model Innovation in Firm Internationalization: A Systematic Literature Review and Future Research Agenda. *Journal of Business Research*, 158, 113659. https://doi.org/10.1016/j.jbusres.2023.113659

Faber, M., Kilic, K., Kozliakov, G., & Marin, D. (2025). *Global Value Chains in a World of Uncertainty and Automation*. SSRN. https://doi.org/10.2139/ssrn.5130665

Farris, D. R., & Sage, A. P. (1975). On the Use of Interpretive Structural Modeling for Worth Assessment. *Computers & Electrical Engineering*, 2(2–3), 149–174. https://doi.org/10.1016/0045-7906(75)90004-X

Faye, M., & Niehaus, P. (2012). Political Aid Cycles. *American Economic Review*, 102(7), 3516–3530. https://doi.org/10.1257/aer.102.7.3516

Feenstra, R., & Hanson, G. (1996). *Globalization, Outsourcing, and Wage Inequality* (No. w5424; p. w5424). National Bureau of Economic Research. https://doi.org/10.3386/w5424

Feng, H., & He, K. (2024). Why Will China and Russia Not Form an Alliance? The Balance of Beliefs in Peacetime. *International Affairs*, 100(5), 2089–2112. https://doi.org/10.1093/ia/iiae184

Ferriani, F., Gazzani, A., & Taboga, M. (2025). The Impact of Trump's Victory on Equity Markets: The Power of Proximity. *Economics Letters*, 247, 112199. https://doi.org/10.1016/j.econlet.2025.112199

Fratocchi, L., Di Mauro, C., Barbieri, P., Nassimbeni, G., & Zanoni, A. (2014). When Manufacturing Moves Back: Concepts and Questions. *Journal of Purchasing and Supply Management*, 20(1), 54–59. https://doi.org/10.1016/j.pursup.2014.01.004

Freund, C., Mattoo, A., Mulabdic, A., & Ruta, M. (2024). Is US Trade Policy Reshaping Global Supply Chains? *Journal of International Economics*, 152, 104011. https://doi.org/10.1016/j.jinteco.2024.104011

Frey, B. S., Luechinger, S., & Stutzer, A. (2007). Calculating Tragedy: Assessing the Costs of Terrorism. *Journal of Economic Surveys*, 21(1), 1–24. https://doi.org/10.1111/j.1467-6419.2007.00505.x

Galston, W. (2020). Efficiency Isn't the Only Economic Virtue. *The Wall Street Journal*. www.wsj.com/articles/efficiency-isnt-the-only-economic-virtue-11583873155

Garcia-Herrero, A. (2022). Slowbalisation in the Context of US-China Decoupling. *Intereconomics*, 57(6), 352–358. https://doi.org/10.1007/s10272-022-1086-x

Gehrke, T., & Medunic, F. (2024). *Fortune Favours the Bold: Upgrading the EU's Geoeconomic Strategy [Policy Brief]*. The European Council on Foreign Relations. https://ecfr.eu/publication/fortune-favours-the-bold-upgrading-the-eus-geoeconomic-strategy/#the-eus-geoeconomic-awakening

Gereffi, G. (2020). What Does the COVID-19 Pandemic Teach Us About Global Value Chains? The Case of Medical Supplies. *Journal of International Business Policy*, 3(3), 287–301. https://doi.org/10.1057/s42214-020-00062-w

Gereffi, G., Humphrey, J., & Sturgeon, T. (2005). The Governance of Global Value Chains. *Review of International Political Economy*, 12(1), 78–104. https://doi.org/10.1080/09692290500049805

Gereffi, G., Lim, H.-C., & Lee, J. (2021). Trade Policies, Firm Strategies, and Adaptive Reconfigurations of Global Value Chains. *Journal of International Business Policy*, 4(4), 506–522. https://doi.org/10.1057/s42214-021-00102-z

Gereffi, G., Posthuma, A. C., & Rossi, A. (2021). Introduction: Disruptions in Global Value Chains – Continuity or Change for Labour Governance?

International Labour Review, 160(4), 501–517. https://doi.org/10.1111/ilr.12333

Ghorbani, Y., Zhang, S. E., Bourdeau, J. E., Chipangamate, N. S., Rose, D. H., Valodia, I., & Nwaila, G. T. (2024). The Strategic Role of Lithium in the Green Energy Transition: Towards an OPEC-Style Framework for Green Energy-Mineral Exporting Countries (GEMEC). *Resources Policy*, 90, 104737. https://doi.org/10.1016/j.resourpol.2024.104737

Global Trade Alert. (2025). *Implementing Juristiction.* GTA Data Center [Data set]. https://globaltradealert.org/data-center?i=616&ki=1&ka=1&ko=0&na=0,999&ast=oneplus&nai=all&kim=1&iis=oneplus&ni=1,999&ke=1&ies=oneplus&nei=all&ky=1&ip=2023-01-01,&kin=0&krn=1&kifd=1&kit=1&kmc=1&kil=1&kef=1&kt=1&kas=1&apit=tree&kap=1&kid=1&kr=1&ij=any&ih=any&cp=2020,2025&tp=2022,2022&td=current&cytd=1&iyd=1&cv=intervention_id&ct=sum&cb=date_implemented_year&type=counts

Gölgeci, I., Yildiz, H. E., & Andersson, U. (2020). The Rising Tensions between Efficiency and Resilience in Global Value Chains in the Post-COVID-19 World. *Transnational Corporations*, 27(2), 127–141. https://doi.org/10.18356/99b1410f-en

Grappi, S., Romani, S., & Bagozzi, R. P. (2018). Reshoring from a Demand-side Perspective: Consumer Reshoring Sentiment and Its Market Effects. *Journal of World Business*, 53(2), 194–208. https://doi.org/10.1016/j.jwb.2017.11.001

Gray, J. V., Esenduran, G., Rungtusanatham, M. J., & Skowronski, K. (2017). Why in the World Did They Reshore? Examining Small to Medium-sized Manufacturer Decisions. *Journal of Operations Management*, 49–51(1), 37–51. https://doi.org/10.1016/j.jom.2017.01.001

Gray, J. V., Skowronski, K., Esenduran, G., & Johnny Rungtusanatham, M. (2013). The Reshoring Phenomenon: What Supply Chain Academics Ought to Know and Should Do. *Journal of Supply Chain Management*, 49(2), 27–33. https://doi.org/10.1111/jscm.12012

Grossman, G. M., & Rossi-Hansberg, E. (2008). Trading Tasks: A Simple Theory of Offshoring. *American Economic Review*, 98(5), 1978–1997. https://doi.org/10.1257/aer.98.5.1978

Grossman, S. J., & Hart, O. D. (1986). The Costs and Benefits of Ownership: A Theory of Vertical and Lateral Integration. *Journal of Political Economy*, 94(4), 691–719. https://doi.org/10.1086/261404

Grubel, H. G., & Lloyd, P. J. (1971). The Empirical Measurement of Intra-Industry Trade*. *Economic Record*, 47(4), 494–517. https://doi.org/10.1111/j.1475-4932.1971.tb00772.x

Guan, C., & Xu, Q. (2021). The Boundary of Supranational Rules: Revisiting Policy Space Conflicts in Global Trade Politics. *Journal of World Trade*, 55(Issue 5), 853–880. https://doi.org/10.54648/TRAD2021036

Guo, Y., Poon, J., Wang, C., & Yang, Y. (2023). China's National Oil Companies Going Global and Coming Home: State–Firm Nexus, Global Financial Networks, and Geopolitical Risks. *Geoforum*, 146, 103880. https://doi.org/10.1016/j.geoforum.2023.103880

Gygli, S., Haelg, F., & Sturm, J.-E. (2018). *The KOF Globalisation Index – Revisited (439)*. KOF Swiss Economic Institute; KOF Working Papers. https://ethz.ch/content/dam/ethz/special-interest/dual/kof-dam/documents/Globalization/2018/KOF_Globalisation%20Index_Revisited.pdf

Hadwick, A. (2023). *Polska w światowych łańcuchach dostaw. Szanse globalne a ryzyka lokalne*. Maersk; Reuters.

Halesiak, A. (2024). *The Bumpy Road of European Re-, On-, and Near-Shoring*. https://andrzejhalesiak.pl/en/the-bumpy-road-of-european-re-on-and-near-shoring/

Haralambides, H. (2023). The State-of-Play in Maritime Economics and Logistics Research (2017–2023). *Maritime Economics & Logistics*, 25(3), 429–451. https://doi.org/10.1057/s41278-023-00265-x

Harvén, S. A. (2023). *he Europe-China Relationship: Dependencies, Divergence and Decoupling*. www.friendsofeurope.org/insights/critical-thinking-the-europe-china-relationship-dependencies-divergence-and-decoupling/

Heiland, I., Moxnes, A., Ulltveit-Moe, K. H., & Zi, Y. (2022). *Trade From Space: Shipping Networks and The Global Implications of Local Shocks* (No. 14193). CEPR Discussion Papers.

Helpman, E., & Krugman, P. (1985). *Market Structure and Foreign Trade Increasing Returns, Imperfect Competition, and the International Economy*. MIT Press.

Hilmola, O.-P., Li, H., Hilletofth, P., & Fjellström, D. (2025). Evaluation of EU-27 Countries as Manufacturing Location: Strengths and Weaknesses Model. *Operations Management Research*. https://doi.org/10.1007/s12063-024-00539-4

Hoekman, B. (2024). Comment on "Can the World Trade Organization Act as a Bulwark Against Deglobalization?" *Asian Economic Policy Review*, 19(1), 60–61. https://doi.org/10.1111/aepr.12448

Hoekman, B. M., Mavroidis, P. C., & Nelson, D. R. (2023). Noneconomic Objectives, Global Value Chains and International Cooperation. *Italian Economic Journal*, 9(3), 1089–1110. https://doi.org/10.1007/s40797-023-00240-8

Hopewell, K. (2025). Unravelling of the Trade Legal Order: Enforcement, Defection and the Crisis of the WTO Dispute Settlement System. *International Affairs*, 101(3), 1103–1117. https://doi.org/10.1093/ia/iiaf055

Hughes, J. (2024). Toward Improved Inference for Krippendorff's Alpha Agreement Coefficient. *Journal of Statistical Planning and Inference*, 233, 106170. https://doi.org/10.1016/j.jspi.2024.106170

Inomata, S. (2017). Analytical frameworks for global value chains: An overview. In *Global Value Chain Development Report 2017*.

Inomata, S., & Hanaka, T. (2024). Measuring exposure to network concentration risk in global supply chains: Volume versus frequency. *Structural Change and Economic Dynamics*, 68, 177–193. https://doi.org/10.1016/j.strueco.2023.10.002

Islam, M. T., & Chadee, D. (2024). Adaptive Governance and Resilience of Global Value Chains: A Framework for Sustaining the Performance of Developing-Country Suppliers during Exogenous Shocks. *International Business Review*, 33(2), 102248. https://doi.org/10.1016/j.ibusrev.2023.102248

Jacobs, J. (2019). Tiptoeing the Line Between National Security and Protectionism: A Comparative Approach to Foreign Direct Investment Screening in the United States and European Union. *International Journal of Legal Information*, 47(02), 105–117. https://doi.org/10.1017/jli.2019.18

Jain, N., Girotra, K., & Netessine, S. (2022). Recovering Global Supply Chains from Sourcing Interruptions: The Role of Sourcing Strategy. *Manufacturing & Service Operations Management*, 24(2), 846–863. https://doi.org/10.1287/msom.2021.0967

Jakubik, A., & Ruta, M. (2023). Trading with Friends in Uncertain Times. *Journal of Policy Modeling*, 45(4), 768–780. https://doi.org/10.1016/j.jpolmod.2023.06.009

Jankowska, B., Mroczek-Dąbrowska, K., Kania, A., & Mińska-Struzik, E. (Eds). (2024). *Emerging Trends of Global Value Chains and Multinational Enterprises in the Pandemic Time*. https://twinseeds.eu/wp-content/uploads/2023/12/WP2-Report.pdf

Jena, J., Fulzele, V., Gupta, R., Sherwani, F., Shankar, R., & Sidharth, S. (2016). A TISM Modeling of Critical Success Factors of Smartphone Manufacturing Ecosystem in India. *Journal of Advances in Management Research*, 13(2), 203–224. https://doi.org/10.1108/JAMR-12-2015-0088

Jensen, N. (2008). Political Risk, Democratic Institutions, and Foreign Direct Investment. *The Journal of Politics*, 70(4), 1040–1052. https://doi.org/10.1017/S0022381608081048

Jiang, C., & Xing, L. (2025). Is China Decoupling from the Global Value Chain? A Quantitative Analysis Framework Based on the Global Production Network. *Humanities and Social Sciences Communications*, 12(1), 796. https://doi.org/10.1057/s41599-025-05183-2

Johnson, R. C., & Noguera, G. (2012). Accounting for Intermediates: Production Sharing and Trade in Value Added. *Journal of International Economics*, 86(2), 224–236. https://doi.org/10.1016/j.jinteco.2011.10.003

Johnstone, P., & Kivimaa, P. (2018). Multiple Dimensions of Disruption, Energy Transitions and Industrial Policy. *Energy Research & Social Science*, 37, 260–265. https://doi.org/10.1016/j.erss.2017.10.027

Kacperska, E. M., Łukasiewicz, K., Skrzypczyk, M., & Stefańczyk, J. (2025). Price Volatility in the European Wheat and Corn Market in the Black Sea Agreement Context. *Agriculture*, 15(1), 91. https://doi.org/10.3390/agriculture15010091

Kano, L., Narula, R., & Surdu, I. (2022). Global Value Chain Resilience: Understanding the Impact of Managerial Governance Adaptations. *California Management Review*, 64(2), 24–45. https://doi.org/10.1177/00081256211066635

Kaushik, A. (2024). Dispute Settlement and Efficacy of the Multilateral Trading System A Dysfunctional Appellate Body Erodes the Credibility of the WTO. *Economic and Political Weekly*, 59(46), 82–88.

Kawashima, F. (2024). Trade Sanctions Against Russia and Their WTO Consistency: Focusing on Justification Under National Security Exceptions. *International Community Law Review*, 26(1–2), 121–150. https://doi.org/10.1163/18719732-12341497

Kazancoglu, Y., Lafci, C., Berberoglu, Y., Upadhyay, A., Rocha-Lona, L., & Kumar, V. (2024). The Effects of Globalization on Supply Chain Resilience: Outsourcing Techniques as Interventionism, Protectionism, and Regionalization Strategies. *Operations Management Research*, 17(2), 505–522. https://doi.org/10.1007/s12063-023-00429-1

Kim, J., Kim, K., Park, S., & Sun, C. (2023). The Economic Costs of Trade Sanctions: Evidence from North Korea. *Journal of International Economics*, 145, 103813. https://doi.org/10.1016/j.jinteco.2023.103813

Klarin, A., & Sosnovskikh, S. (2024). Leveraging Friendshoring in Response to Sanctions: Essential Insights for Global Managers. *Business Horizons*, S0007681324001435. https://doi.org/10.1016/j.bushor.2024.10.002

Kobrin, S. J. (2017). Bricks and Mortar in a Borderless World: Globalization, the Backlash, and the Multinational Enterprise. *Global Strategy Journal*, 7(2), 159–171. https://doi.org/10.1002/gsj.1158

Kong, Q., Yamada, M., Yang, C., & Nie, H. (2025). Competition or Complementarity? Assessing the Interaction Effects of RCEP and CPTPP on Agricultural and Non-Agricultural Trade Flows. *International Economics and Economic Policy*, 22(1), 7. https://doi.org/10.1007/s10368-024-00628-6

Krasner, S. D. (1976). State Power and the Structure of International Trade. *World Politics*, 28(3), 317–347. https://doi.org/10.2307/2009974

Krenz, A., Prettner, K., & Strulik, H. (2021). Robots, Reshoring, and the Lot of Low-Skilled Workers. *European Economic Review*, 136, 103744. https://doi.org/10.1016/j.euroecorev.2021.103744

Krenz, A., & Strulik, H. (2021). Quantifying Reshoring at the Macro-Level—Measurement and Applications. *Growth and Change*, 52(3), 1200–1229. https://doi.org/10.1111/grow.12513

Krykavskyy, Y., Shandrivska, O., & Pawłyszyn, I. (2023). A Study of Macroeconomic and Geopolitical Influences and Security Risks in Supply Chains in Times of Disrup. *Logforum*, 19(3), 423–441. https://doi.org/10.17270/J.LOG.2023.855

Lee, H.-C., & Chang, C.-T. (2018). Comparative Analysis of MCDM Methods for Ranking Renewable Energy Sources in Taiwan. *Renewable and Sustainable Energy Reviews*, 92, 883–896. https://doi.org/10.1016/j.rser.2018.05.007

Lei, Y., & Sui, S. (2024). China–Russia Strategic Partnership and the Oil and Gas collaboration. *Innovation: The European Journal of Social Science Research*, 37(4), 1224–1243. https://doi.org/10.1080/13511610.2023.2289827

Li, Q., & Vashchilko, T. (2010). Dyadic Military Conflict, Security Alliances, and Bilateral FDI Flows. *Journal of International Business Studies*, 41(5), 765–782. https://doi.org/10.1057/jibs.2009.91

Liou, J. J. H., Wang, H. S., Hsu, C. C., & Yin, S. L. (2011). A Hybrid Model for Selection of an Outsourcing Provider. *Applied Mathematical Modelling*, 35(10), 5121–5133. https://doi.org/10.1016/j.apm.2011.04.020

Liu, Y., Jin, X., & Zhang, Y. (2024). Identifying Risks in Temporal Supernetworks: An IO-SuperPageRank Algorithm. *Humanities and Social Sciences Communications*, 11(1), 306. https://doi.org/10.1057/s41599-024-02823-x

Low, P. (2011). *WTO Decision-Making for the Future*. World Trade Organization. www.wto.org/english/res_e/reser_e/ersd201105_e.pdf

Lu, B., & Liu, W. (2024). Does Comprehensive Geopolitical Risk Deter FDI Outflows: Evidence from China. *Defence and Peace Economics*, 35(3), 383–399. https://doi.org/10.1080/10242694.2022.2160140

Luo, Y. (2022). Illusions of Techno-Nationalism. *Journal of International Business Studies*, 53(3), 550–567. https://doi.org/10.1057/s41267-021-00468-5

Luo, Y. (2024). Paradigm Shift and Theoretical Implications for the Era of Global Disorder. *Journal of International Business Studies*, 55(2), 127–135. https://doi.org/10.1057/s41267-023-00659-2

Luo, Y., & Van Assche, A. (2023). The Rise of Techno-Geopolitical Uncertainty: Implications of the United States CHIPS and Science Act. *Journal of International Business Studies*, 54(8), 1423–1440. https://doi.org/10.1057/s41267-023-00620-3

Luo, Y., & Witt, M. A. (2022). Springboard MNEs Under De-globalization. *Journal of International Business Studies*, 53(4), 767–780. https://doi.org/10.1057/s41267-021-00423-4

Mariano, S., & Laker, B. (2024). On-the-Fly Decision Making Within Organizations: A Systematic Literature Review and Future Research

Directions. *Journal of Business Research*, 174, 114484. https://doi.org/10.1016/j.jbusres.2023.114484

Mariotti, S. (2024a). "Open Strategic Autonomy" as an Industrial Policy Compass for the EU Competitiveness and Growth: The Good, the Bad, or the Ugly? *Journal of Industrial and Business Economics*. https://doi.org/10.1007/s40812-024-00327-y

Mariotti, S. (2024b). "Win-lose" Globalization and the Weaponization of Economic Policies by Nation-States. *Critical Perspectives on International Business*, 20(5), 638–659. https://doi.org/10.1108/cpoib-09-2023-0089

Martin, J., Mejean, I., & Parenti, M. (2023). Relationship Stickiness, International Trade, and Economic Uncertainty. *Review of Economics and Statistics*, 1–45. https://doi.org/10.1162/rest_a_01396

Matysek-Jędrych, A., Mroczek-Dąbrowska, K., & Kania, A. (2022). Beyond the COVID-19 Pandemic: What Builds Organizational Resilience Capacity? *International Journal of Emerging Markets*. https://doi.org/10.1108/IJOEM-06-2022-0948

Melitz, M. (2003). The Impact of Trade on Intra-Industry Reallocations and Aggregate Industry Productivity. *Econometrica*, 71(6), 1695–1725.

Meunier, S., & Nicolaidis, K. (2019). The Geopoliticization of European Trade and Investment Policy. *JCMS: Journal of Common Market Studies*, 57(S1), 103–113. https://doi.org/10.1111/jcms.12932

Miles, M., & Huberman, M. (1994). *Qualitative Data Analysis: A Sourcebook of New Methods*. Sage.

Miller, C. (2022). *Chip War: The Fight for the World's Most Critical Technology*. Simon & Schuster Ltd.

Miró, J. (2023). Responding to the Global Disorder: The EU's Quest for Open Strategic Autonomy. *Global Society*, 37(3), 315–335. https://doi.org/10.1080/13600826.2022.2110042

Mohamad, A. (2024). Herding Behaviour Surrounding the Russo–Ukraine War and COVID-19 Pandemic: Evidence from Energy, Metal, Livestock and Grain Commodities. *Review of Behavioral Finance*, 16(5), 925–957. https://doi.org/10.1108/RBF-12-2023-0339

Morão, H. (2025). Fuel Price Surges and Rising Inflation Expectations in the Euro Area. *International Economics*, 181, 100576. https://doi.org/10.1016/j.inteco.2024.100576

Mroczek-Dąbrowska, K., Cherubin, D., & Kania, A. (2024). The Art of Deception: The Trade-off between the Information Distortion and Perception of FDI Location Attractiveness. *Business and Economics Review,* 12(3). https://doi.org/10.15678/EBER.2024.120311

Mroczek-Dąbrowska, K., & Jędrych-Matysek, A. (2022). Brexit Aftermath—A Lot of Fuss Over Nothing? The Perspective of the EU-27 Member States. *International Journal of Economic Policy in Emerging Economies*, 15(1), 28. https://doi.org/10.1504/IJEPEE.2022.120060

Mroczek-Dąbrowska, K., Schartinger, D., Jankowska, B., Kania, A., Götz, M., Orsulic, A., & Dachs, B. (2024). *Agile Reshoring as a New Answer to Challenges in the Era of Disruptions*. SSRN. https://doi.org/10.2139/ssrn.5061149

Notteboom, T., Haralambides, H., & Cullinane, K. (2024). The Red Sea Crisis: Ramifications for Vessel Operations, Shipping Networks, and Maritime Supply Chains. *Maritime Economics & Logistics*, 26(1), 1–20. https://doi.org/10.1057/s41278-024-00287-z

OECD. (2019). *Global Material Resources Outlook to 2060: Economic Drivers and Environmental Consequences*. OECD. https://doi.org/10.1787/9789264307452-en

Olsthoorn, K. (2024). The EU's Anti-coercion Instrument: A Return of Unlawful Unilateral Trade Countermeasures in Disguise? *Legal Issues of Economic Integration*, 51(Issue 1), 47–86. https://doi.org/10.54648/LEIE2024003

Pahis, S. (2024). Appeals after the Appellate Body. *World Trade Review*, 23(3), 296–323. https://doi.org/10.1017/S1474745624000041

Pananond, P., Gereffi, G., & Pedersen, T. (2020). An Integrative Typology of Global Strategy and Global Value Chains: The Management and Organization of Cross-Border Activities. *Global Strategy Journal*, 10(3), 421–443. https://doi.org/10.1002/gsj.1388

Park, S. A. (2023). Shifted Paradigm in Technonationalism in the 21st Century: The Influence of Global Value Chain (GVC) and US-China Competition on International Politics and Global Commerce —A Case Study of Japan's Semiconductor Industry. *Asia and the Global Economy*, 3(2), 100063. https://doi.org/10.1016/j.aglobe.2023.100063

Pedersen, T., Jensen, P. Ø., Busck-Lumholt, L. M., Canello, J., Ghodsi, M., Landesmann, M., Francis, S., Los, B., Capello, R., Dellisanti, R., Ando, M., Hayakawa, K., Kimura, F., & Resmini, L. (2024). *Recent and Emerging Impact of GVCs and MNEs on Growth, Productivity and Competitiveness*. https://twinseeds.eu/wp-content/uploads/2024/11/WP5-Report.pdf

Pedroletti, D. (2025). Network Effects of Partial Reshoring in the Internationalization process. *International Business Review*, 102401. https://doi.org/10.1016/j.ibusrev.2025.102401

Pedroletti, D., & Ciabuschi, F. (2023). Reshoring: A Review and Research Agenda. *Journal of Business Research*, 164, 114005. https://doi.org/10.1016/j.jbusres.2023.114005

Pegoraro, D., De Propris, L., & Chidlow, A. (2022). Regional Factors Enabling Manufacturing Reshoring Strategies: A Case Study Perspective. *Journal of International Business Policy,* 5(1), 112–133. https://doi.org/10.1057/s42214-021-00112-x

Pettit, T. J., Fiksel, J., & Croxton, K. L. (2010). Ensuring Supply Chain Resilience: Development of a Conceptual Framework. *Journal of Business Logistics*, 31(1), 1–21. https://doi.org/10.1002/j.2158-1592.2010.tb00125.x

Piatanesi, B., & Arauzo-Carod, J. (2019). Backshoring and Nearshoring: An Overview. *Growth and Change*, 50(3), 806–823. https://doi.org/10.1111/grow.12316

Piserà, S., Paltrinieri, A., Galletta, S., & Pichler, F. (2025). Trump's Tariffs: Unpacking the EU's Market Reaction. *Economics Letters*, 252, 112380. https://doi.org/10.1016/j.econlet.2025.112380

Ploom, I., Kalvet, T., & Tiits, M. (2022). Defence Industries in Small European States: Key Contemporary Challenges and Opportunities. *Journal Of International Studies*, 15(4), 112–130. https://doi.org/10.14254/2071-8330.2022/15-4/7

Podsakoff, P. M., MacKenzie, S. B., Bachrach, D. G., & Podsakoff, N. P. (2005). The Influence of Management Journals in the 1980s and 1990s. *Strategic Management Journal*, 26(5), 473–488. https://doi.org/10.1002/smj.454

Ponte, S. (2002). The 'Latte Revolution'? Regulation, Markets and Consumption in the Global Coffee Chain. *World Development*, 30(7), 1099–1122. https://doi.org/10.1016/S0305-750X(02)00032-3

Porter, M. E. (1985). *Competitive Advantage, Creating and Sustaining Superior Performance*. Free Press.

Pushp, P., Sharma, A., & Ahmed, F. (2024). Flexibility in the WTO: Navigating the Dynamics of Multilateralism Using Grounded Theory. *Global Journal of Flexible Systems Management*, 25(4), 805–823. https://doi.org/10.1007/s40171-024-00413-z

Pye, S., Bradshaw, M., Price, J., Zhang, D., Kuzemko, C., Sharples, J., Welsby, D., & Dodds, P. E. (2025). The Global Implications of a Russian Gas Pivot to Asia. *Nature Communications*, 16(1), 386. https://doi.org/10.1038/s41467-024-55697-7

Qianyi, S. (2025). Impact of China's Accession Protocol on Its Participation in the WTO Dispute Settlement Mechanism: An Analysis of Eleven Cases Involving China's Accession Protocol. *Heliyon*, 11(1), e39886. https://doi.org/10.1016/j.heliyon.2024.e39886

Rai, S. S., Rai, S., & Singh, N. K. (2021). Organizational Resilience and Social-Economic Sustainability: COVID-19 Perspective. *Environment, Development and Sustainability*, 23(8), 12006–12023. https://doi.org/10.1007/s10668-020-01154-6

Reshoring Initiative 2022 Data Report. (2023). Reshoring Initiative. https://reshorenow.org/blog/reshoring-initiative-2021-data-report/

Righetti, E., Rizos, V., & Moreschi, M. (2025). *Setting Standards for Critical Raw Materials. State of Play and Future Prospects*. Centre for European Policy Studies. https://cdn.ceps.eu/wp-content/uploads/2025/01/2025-02_ERCC_Raw-Materials-Standardisation.pdf

Rimmer, M. (2024). The Regional Comprehensive Economic Partnership: Intellectual Property and Trade in the Asia-Pacific. *Asia*

Pacific Law Review, 32(2), 392–435. https://doi.org/10.1080/10192557.2024.2349387

Riti, J. S., Shu, Y., & Riti, M.-K. J. (2022). Geopolitical Risk and Environmental Degradation in BRICS: Aggregation Bias and Policy Inference. *Energy Policy*, 166, 113010. https://doi.org/10.1016/j.enpol.2022.113010

Robinson, P. K., & Hsieh, L. (2016). Reshoring: A Strategic Renewal of Luxury Clothing Supply Chains. *Operations Management Research*, 9(3–4), 89–101. https://doi.org/10.1007/s12063-016-0116-x

Rodgers, P. (2024). Failure of Red Sea Coalition and Downfall of US Hegemony – OpEd. *Eurasia Review*. www.eurasiareview.com/22042024-failure-of-red-sea-coalition-and-downfall-of-us-hegemony-oped/

Rodriguez, C., Ciravegna, L., & Petersen, B. (2023). Geographical Reconfiguration in Global Value Chains: Search Within Limited Space? *Global Strategy Journal*, 13(2), 440–482. https://doi.org/10.1002/gsj.1441

Rodrik, D. (2011). *The Globalization Paradox: Democracy and the Future of the World Economy*. W. W. Norton & Company.

Rushton, C. (2024). *Nearshoring: Home Truths*. Savills. www.savills.com/impacts/market-trends/nearshoring-home-truths.html

Saeidi, R., Noorollahi, Y., Aghaz, J., & Chang, S. (2023). FUZZY-TOPSIS Method for Defining Optimal Parameters and Finding Suitable Sites for PV Power Plants. *Energy*, 282, 128556. https://doi.org/10.1016/j.energy.2023.128556

Sahoo, S., Kumar, S., Mukherjee, D., Kraus, S., Dabić, M., & Mahto, R. V. (2024). Internationalization via Industry 4.0 Technologies: Application Areas and Future Roadmap for International Business. *Management Review Quarterly*. https://doi.org/10.1007/s11301-024-00459-4

Schmeisser, B. (2013). A Systematic Review of Literature on Offshoring of Value Chain Activities. *Journal of International Management*, 19(4), 390–406. https://doi.org/10.1016/j.intman.2013.03.011

Seidl, T., & Schmitz, L. (2024). Moving on to Not Fall Behind? Technological Sovereignty and the 'Geo-Dirigiste' Turn in EU Industrial Policy. *Journal of European Public Policy*, 31(8), 2147–2174. https://doi.org/10.1080/13501763.2023.2248204

Sekliuckiene, J., & Rybakovas, E. (2023). The Quest for Regionalization of Global Value Chains in a Pandemic Global Business Environment. *Engineering Economics*, 34(2), 230–239. https://doi.org/10.5755/j01.ee.34.2.31640

Seong, J., White, O., Birshan, M., Woetzel, L., Lamanna, C., Condon, J., & Devesa, T. (2024). *Geopolitics and the Geometry of Global Trade*. McKinsey Global Insitute. file:///C:/Users/USER/Downloads/geopolitics-and-the-geometry-of-global-trade-vf.pdf

Seyfi, S., & Hall, C. M. (2020). Sanctions and Tourism: Effects, Complexities and Research. *Tourism Geographies*, 22(4–5), 749–767. https://doi.org/10.1080/14616688.2019.1663911

Shadlen, K. (2008). Globalisation, Power and Integration: The Political Economy of Regional and Bilateral Trade Agreements in the Americas. *The Journal of Development Studies*, 44(1), 1–20. https://doi.org/10.1080/13562570701722089

Solingen, E., Meng, B., & Xu, A. (2021). *Rising Risks to Global Value Chains*. World Trade Organization.

Sorooshian, S., Tavana, M., & Ribeiro-Navarrete, S. (2023). From classical interpretive structural modeling to total interpretive structural modeling and beyond: A half-century of business research. *Journal of Business Research*, 157, 113642. https://doi.org/10.1016/j.jbusres.2022.113642

Soylu, R. (2024). Turkey, Iraq, Qatar and UAE sign transportation deal that hopes to connect Gulf to Europe. *Middle East Eye*. www.middleeasteye.net/news/turkey-iraq-qatar-and-uae-sign-transportation-deal-would-connect-gulf-europe

Stamer, V. (2024). *Trump's Tariffs – Who Really Loses Out?* Economic Research. www.commerzbank.de/group/research/week-in-focus/wif2211e.pdf

Stöllinger, R., Hanzl-Weiss, D., Leitner, S., & Stehrer, R. (2018). *Global and Regional Value Chains: How Important, How Different?* The Vienna Institute for International Economic Studies. https://wiiw.ac.at/global-and-regio-nal-value-chainshow-important-how-different--dlp-4522.pdf

Strange, R., & Humphrey, J. (2019). What Lies between Market and Hierarchy? Insights from Internalization Theory and Global Value Chain Theory. *Journal of International Business Studies*, 50(8), 1401–1413. https://doi.org/10.1057/s41267-018-0186-0

Strauss, A., & Corbin, J. (1998). *Basics of Qualitative Research: Techniques and Procedures for Developing Grounded Theory*. Sage.

Supply Chain Management Insights. (2023). Deloitte. file:///C:/Users/USER/Downloads/CE-CFO-2023-Report-Supply-Chain-Management.pdf

Sushil. (2017). Modified ISM/TISM Process with Simultaneous Transitivity Checks for Reducing Direct Pair Comparisons. *Global Journal of Flexible Systems Management*, 18(4), 331–351. https://doi.org/10.1007/s40171-017-0167-3

Taira, S. (2024). WTO Dispute Settlement and Trade Sanctions as Permissible Third-Party Countermeasures Under Customary International Law. In M. Asada & D. Tamada (Eds), *The War in Ukraine and International Law* (pp. 185–216). Springer Nature Singapore. https://doi.org/10.1007/978-981-97-2504-5_8

Tinti, E. (2025). Open Strategic Autonomy, FDI Screening and Industrial Policy: What Geopolitical Role for the European Commission? In J. H. Pohl, S. Hindelang, T. Papadopoulos, & J. Wiesenthal (Eds), *The Law and Geoeconomics of Investment Screening* (Vol. 4, pp. 205–228). Springer Nature Switzerland. https://doi.org/10.1007/978-3-031-75554-5_9

Townsend, S. (2024). Cost of Red Sea Shipping Insurance Rises 2,700%. *Arabian Gulf Business Insight*. www.agbi.com/logistics/2024/02/cost-of-red-sea-shipping-insurance-rises-20-fold/

Tranfield, D., Denyer, D., & Smart, P. (2003). Towards a Methodology for Developing Evidence-Informed Management Knowledge by Means of Systematic Review. *British Journal of Management*, 14(3), 207–222. https://doi.org/10.1111/1467-8551.00375

Tung, R. L., Zander, I., & Fang, T. (2023). The Tech Cold War, the Multipolarization of the World Economy, and IB Research. *International Business Review*, 32(6), 102195. https://doi.org/10.1016/j.ibusrev.2023.102195

Van Assche, A. (2025). Honoring Yadong Luo: Contributions to Geopolitics and International Business. *Asia Pacific Journal of Management*, 42(1), 31–41. https://doi.org/10.1007/s10490-025-10016-6

Van Meeteren, M., & Kleibert, J. (2022). The Global Division of Labour as Enduring Archipelago: Thinking through the Spatiality of 'Globalisation in Reverse'. *Cambridge Journal of Regions, Economy and Society,* 15(2), 389–406. https://doi.org/10.1093/cjres/rsac007

Van Meijl, H., Bartelings, H., Van Berkum, S., Cui, H. D., Kristkova, Z. S., & Van Zeist, W. J. (2024). The Russia-Ukraine War Decreases Food Affordability But Could Reduce Global Greenhouse Gas Emissions. *Communications Earth & Environment,* 5(1), 59. https://doi.org/10.1038/s43247-024-01208-x

Vissak, T., & Francioni, B. (2013). Serial Nonlinear Internationalization in Practice: A Case Study. *International Business Review*, 22(6), 951–962. https://doi.org/10.1016/j.ibusrev.2013.01.010

Visser, M., Van Eck, N. J., & Waltman, L. (2021). Large-Scale Comparison of Bibliographic Data Sources: Scopus, Web of Science, Dimensions, Crossref, and Microsoft Academic. *Quantitative Science Studies,* 2(1), 20–41. https://doi.org/10.1162/qss_a_00112

Waller, M. A. (2001). Resilience in Ecosystemic Context: Evolution of the Concept. *American Journal of Orthopsychiatry*, 71(3), 290–297. https://doi.org/10.1037/0002-9432.71.3.290

Webber, D. (2016). Declining Power Europe: The Evolution of the European Union's World Power in the Early 21st Century. *European Review of International Studies*, 3(1), 31–52.

Weber, P. M., & Stępień, B. (2020). Conform or Challenge? Adjustment Strategies of Sanction-torn Companies. *The World Economy*, 43(11), 3006–3024. https://doi.org/10.1111/twec.12985

Wendt, A. (1992). Anarchy Is What States Make of It: The Social Construction of Power Politics. *International Organization*, 46(2), 391–425. https://doi.org/10.1017/S0020818300027764

Wengerek, S. T., Uhde, A., & Hippert, B. (2025). Share Price Reactions to Tariff Imposition Announcements during the First Trump Administration. *Finance Research Letters*, 80, 107381. https://doi.org/10.1016/j.frl.2025.107381

Wernick, D. A. (2006). Terror Incognito: International Business in an Era of Heightened Geopolitical Risk. In G. G. S. Suder (Ed), *Corporate Strategies under International Terrorism and Adversity*. Edward Elgar Publishing. https://doi.org/10.4337/9781847200228.00015

Wigger, A. (2023). The New EU Industrial Policy and Deepening Structural Asymmetries: Smart Specialisation Not So Smart. *JCMS: Journal of Common Market Studies*, 61(1), 20–37. https://doi.org/10.1111/jcms.13366

Witt, M. A. (2019). De-globalization: Theories, Predictions, and Opportunities for International Business Research. *Journal of International Business Studies*, 50(7), 1053–1077. https://doi.org/10.1057/s41267-019-00219-7

Witt, M. A., Lewin, A. Y., Li, P. P., & Gaur, A. (2023). Decoupling in International Business: Evidence, Drivers, Impact, and Implications for IB Research. *Journal of World Business*, 58(1), 101399. https://doi.org/10.1016/j.jwb.2022.101399

World Economic Forum. (2024). *From Disruption to Opportunity: Strategies for Rewiring Global Value Chains*. https://www3.weforum.org/docs/WEF_From_Disruption_to_Opportunity_2024.pdf

World Investment Report 2020. International Production Beyond the Pandemic. (2020). UNCTAD. https://unctad.org/en/PublicationsLibrary/wir2020_en.pdf

World Investment Report 2023. (2024). United Nations. https://unctad.org/system/files/official-document/wir2023_en.pdf

Yang, C., & Chan, D. Y.-T. (2023). Geopolitical Risks of Strategic Decoupling and Recoupling in the Mobile Phone Production Shift from China to Vietnam: Evidence from the Sino-US Trade War and COVID-19 Pandemic. *Applied Geography*, 158, 103028. https://doi.org/10.1016/j.apgeog.2023.103028

Yang, Y., & Dong, W. (2016). Global Energy Networks: Insights from Headquarter Subsidiary Data of Transnational Petroleum Corporations. *Applied Geography*, 72, 36–46. https://doi.org/10.1016/j.apgeog.2016.05.003

Yap, D. Y. P. (2024). Developing Country Status in the WTO: Investigating Self-Designation and Perpetuation of the "Pretend" Culture. *Journal of International Trade Law and Policy*, 23(1), 1–13. https://doi.org/10.1108/JITLP-01-2023-0003

Yesilcayir, N., Ayvazoglu, G., Celik, S., & Peker, I. (2024). Transit Warehouse Location Selection by IF AHP- TOPSIS Integrated Methods for Disaster Logistics: A Case Study of Turkey. *Research in Transportation Business & Management*, 57, 101232. https://doi.org/10.1016/j.rtbm.2024.101232

Zachariadis, I. (2019). *Global and Regional Value Chains. Opportunities for European SMEs' Internationalisation and Growth*. European Parliamentary Research Service. www.europarl.europa.eu/RegData/etudes/BRIE/2019/635520/EPRS_BRI(2019)635520_EN.pdf

Zeng, K., & Kim, S. Y. (2024). Chinese Firms in the US–China Trade War: Decoupling through Reshoring? *International Studies Quarterly*, 69(1), sqae117. https://doi.org/10.1093/isq/sqae117

Zhao, G., Li, W., Geng, Y., & Bleischwitz, R. (2023). Uncovering the Features of Global Antimony Resource Trade Network. *Resources Policy*, 85, 103815. https://doi.org/10.1016/j.resourpol.2023.103815

Index

Note: Page numbers in *italics* refer to figures, and those in **bold** refer to tables.

For Product Safety Concerns and Information please contact our EU
representative GPSR@taylorandfrancis.com Taylor & Francis Verlag GmbH,
Kaufingerstraße 24, 80331 München, Germany

Printed and bound by CPI Group (UK) Ltd, Croydon, CR0 4YY
14/09/2026
02216256-0005